THE PUBS OF RYE, EAST SUSSEX

1750–1950

BY THE SAME AUTHOR

The Pubs of Hastings & St Leonards 1800–2000

Register of Licensees for Hastings & St Leonards 1500–2010

The Swan, Hastings 1523–1943

The Pubs of Hastings & St Leonards 1800–2000 Second Edition

THE PUBS OF RYE, EAST SUSSEX

1750–1950

◇————————◇

DAVID RUSSELL

Including photographs from the
John Hodges archive

Published by Lynda Russell

Copies of this book are available from the publisher
Email: hastings.pubs@gmail.com
Tel: 01424 200227
www.hastingspubhistory.com

Printed and bound by Imprint Digital.net, Exeter
ISBN 978-0-9562917-4-5

Front cover: Water colour of the Ferry Boat Inn
by Jean Hope, Hastings

Contents

Acknowledgements

I would like to acknowledge the assistance and skills of the staff of Hastings Reference Library, Rye Public Library and the East Sussex Records Office, Lewes.

The water colour of the Ferry Boat Inn on the front cover is the work of Jean Hope, Hastings.

The photographs on pages 12, 13, 19, 33, 39, 47, 75, 80, 83, 89, 95, 100, 102, 107, 111, 121, 127, 165, 175, 183, 199, 207, 209, 215 and 262 are the property of John Hodges and are taken from the John Hodges photographic archive.

The photographs on pages 25, 27, 32, 53, 54, 62, 63, 64, 71, 82, 94, 108, 113, 120, 126, 132, 138, 144, 151, 152, 158, 166, 170, 173, 182, 189, 190, 200, 203, 206, 214, 222, 230 and 236 are attributed to Lynda Russell.

All other photographs are available on the internet.

I would also like to acknowledge Arthur Taylor and Patrick Chaplin for information on Spinning Jenny and the Wheel of Fortune.

Above all I would like to thank my wife Lynda for all her hard work designing, editing and publishing this book. Without her skills and dedication it would not have seen the light of day.

Introduction

In 1750, the start of my period of investigation, it is estimated that there were 13 inns and alehouses in the town of Rye. Over the next eight years this number was reduced to seven when the Flushing Inn, Mermaid, Ship in Distress, Bull Head, Hoy and the Fortune had all closed by 1758. This left only the George, Red Lion, London Trader, Two Brewers, Rye Galley, (the first) Ferry Boat and the Dolphin.

In 1750 Rye's population was about 2,000 which meant that the ratio of licensed premises to the population was about one pub to every 166 people. However, in the context of poor quality drinking water where nearly everyone was dependant to some extent on (table) beer there were certainly a number of unlicensed drinking places, as well as the traditional brewster women who brewed and sold beer for a living from their homes and in the streets.

When the Dolphin on the Gun Garden closed in 1801 the number of licensed premises was reduced to six. According to the census of that year the population was now 2,145, which meant that the pub/population ratio had jumped to 1:350. Obviously demand on the publican had increased.

This must have been a trying period for licensees. The local population, which was growing slowly, was swelled during the turbulent times of the Napoleonic Wars when troops were billeted in warehouses on the Strand and elsewhere, whilst the number of pubs had fallen. The ratio between the population and its licensed premises then became even higher. This was only marginally offset when the number of pubs was increased to seven with the building and opening of the Cinque Ports Arms in Rope Walk, now Cinque Ports Street, in 1820.

By 1821 the population had risen to 3,600 and we can only imagine the crowded conditions in the local bars and taprooms. The policy of the local licensing magistrates seems to have been one of keeping pub numbers down and demand up. Local brewers, licensees and magistrates unofficially acted together as an oligarchy for their own purposes, and consequently those lucky enough to have a licence did lucrative business.

This fundamental fact changed with the introduction of the 1830 Beer Act by the unpopular Wellington government. Under this Act a ratepayer could, on the payment of two guineas, get a licence to sell beer (but not wine or spirits) direct from the Excise. This new method of obtaining a licence bypassed the local magistrates and quickly reduced their monopoly powers.

Following the 1830 Act and the 'free trade in beer' as it became known, a number of beer houses immediately opened up in the town. Just how many we have yet to ascertain but the Jolly Sailor, William IV, and the Greyhound were just three of many from that time. Most of the new licensees eventually applied for a full licence and several beer houses which survived this period are still in business. The magistrates felt that by granting a beer house a full licence, it would then come under their authority and control. Their thinking seems to have been 'better the devil you control than the one you don't'!

Between 1830 and 1872 when the law changed yet again, pub numbers increased. The high point came at the end of the 1860s when Rye had 28 pubs; reduced to 27 when the Red Lion was destroyed by fire in 1872.

The sting in the tail came with a further Act in 1904 which gave the police powers to recommend closure of 'redundant pubs', which they did with indecent haste to the delight of the temperance movement and local churches.

Between 1904 and 1911 eight pubs were closed down in this way, and another, the Swan, was volunteered for closure by the Edwin Finn Brewery of Lydd, making a total of nine. By 1909 all of Rye's old beer houses had gone and the number of pubs stood at 16. In the inter-war period the pub/population ratio was, according to the chief constable's own figures, 1:190. This was not too different from Hastings (1:128) but very different from Eastbourne (1:574) or Blackpool (1:711), for example.

The Rye magistrates were very aware of this ratio and, heavily influenced by the changed conditions of the licensed trade in the First World War and by the temperance movement, were to remain so until after the Second World War. Temperance lobbying ensured there were no new licences granted between 1870 and 1955. This had serious consequences for the famous Mermaid, which was only re-licensed without restrictions in the latter year.

Because of boundary changes in 1935 the total number of public houses increased from 15 to 16 when the Kings Head, Rye Hill was included in the borough of Rye. This total reverted back to 15 with the bombing of the Cinque Ports Arms in 1943.

What follows is the history of 32 Rye pubs (and one cinema) which existed at sometime between 1750 and 1950. Four other pubs, the Hoy, the Fortune, the Ship in Distress and the Rye Galley are not included because of poor information.

This history is supported by five appendices. Appendix one is a register of licensees and a list of 59 licensed premises known to date. Other appendices provide information on the local friendly societies, the Rye temperance movement, the Treating Scandal of 1852 and the mock mayor elections in the 19th century.

Ship builders, hop pickers, mariners, fishermen, smugglers, the Home Guard, bonfire boys, prostitutes, friendly societies, mock mayors, gamblers, a peruke maker and yes, even temperance campaigners can all be found in and around the inns, alehouses and pubs of Rye. A few stories about murder and political corruption thrown in with the odd ghost, surely makes *The Pubs of Rye, East Sussex* a good read.

David Russell, St Leonards-on-Sea, October 2012

Kings Head, Rye Hill
included in the borough of Rye 1935

Bedford Arms
Fishmarket Road

1970s

The initials 'W A' on Rye pottery in the early 19th century, stand for the name William Apps. There were three generations of clay pipe makers with this name in Rye, and all marked their products 'W A'. The last of the three pipe makers was also the first landlord of the Bedford Arms.

In 1835 William Apps 'the younger', clay pipe maker and Town Clerk, took a lease 'on a piece of waste ground without Landgate on the east side of the common highway and town Salts', where the Bedford Arms now stands. The lease was for 99 years at an annual rent of £3. 13s [£3.65p]. The common highway, now Fishmarket Road, is the street of small houses, a pub and the open space that you see today. The Bedford Arms was built by William Apps, or more likely converted from one or more of the cottages.[1]

In 1848 a new lease was assigned to George Dann, described as a 'yeoman', or market gardener. He was previously landlord of another public house the Barley Mow in Landgate, and became the second licensee of the Bedford Arms in the early 1850s.

By 1850 the Bedford was owned by James Batchelor, ale and porter brewer of Landgate Brewery, King Street later Bowen's Brewery, Rye.

In 1853 George Dann purchased the Bedford Arms outright from the brewery with a mortgage for £300. In 1856 he also purchased the freehold of a nearby warehouse used for storing wool gathered from Romney Marsh sheep. Farmers, shepherds and employees of the warehouse were all early customers of the Bedford Arms, whose licence was now held by William Relf.[2]

From 1861 William Relf was requested by Rye Corporation 'to be so good as to give twelve petty jurymen refreshment to the extent of one shilling each', after they had sat on a jury for a number of hours.[3]

At this time the Albion Benefit Society had about 20 members and the Triennial Benefit Society about 15. These two societies, formerly one society called the Albion, were established in 1837 at the Queen Adelaide, but in 1861 the Albion transferred to the Bedford Arms Inn and the Triennial to the Crown.

By the mid-19th century, the Bedford drew most of its custom from those living and working on Romney Marsh and around Rye Harbour. Before 1872 when pub opening times were changed, the

Bedford opened early in the morning to serve rum and milk to local fishermen returning from a night's fishing.

But Bedford custom also came from a much larger source; the hop farms in the surrounding countryside. For many years from the 1840s, several Rye pubs were patronised by hop pickers. From early September through to October the Bedford Arms, the Queen Adelaide, the London Stout House, the Kings Arms and the Ship, were some of the many pubs used by pickers during the hop season. The following sketch by a local reporter is of a typical hoppers evening in the pub in the 1870s:

AMONG THE HOPPERS

The day's labour is done, the hopper sets forth in search of his amusement .... With his dirt thick upon him, away he trudges to the nearest public house or beer house. In some instances he is accompanied by a female companion, but it is too early for the women yet, they will put in an appearance by and bye. We arrive at the house. My ears tell me that several of the fraternity are before us. We enter the taproom. Early as it is the place is already filled with smoke.

I take my place at one of the tables and await events. A half an-hour or so elapses and in come the women, in some cases accompanied by children. I am among a strange crew, but I am determined to make myself at home as much as I possibly can. I fraternise with my associates. I get behind a short clay pipe and puff my tobacco. I purchase the friendship of one or two in my immediate vicinity by 'standing' a jug or two of beer.

I have time to study the characters of my new friends. What capacious stomachs they have, with what extraordinary facility the beer disappears! They are becoming noisy, but not yet pugnacious. Now we are packed closely — crowding, in fact, one upon another. The door opens, and in tumbles an addition to the party, who is at once greeted with "Hallo, Frenchey", "Here's Frenchey", "Frenchey, my tulip, tip us your fins".

It is evident at a glance that Frenchey has been imbibing somewhat freely. Curious to know why he attracts so much attention, I go and sit beside him. I discover that he is a foreigner. I muster up my small stock of French and try a conversation. Frenchey turns out to be a German. I declare the fact; the hoppers are amazed and express their wonderment. I invite my foreign friend to drink with me. He accepts and for the remainder of the evening I am addressed by him as mon officier — for Frenchey knows a little French and I know no German.

I turn the conversation to the war [the Franco-Prussian War: 1870]. However, he shirks the question. I ask him why he, a young man, does not take up arms amongst the brethren of his nation. He tells me he prefers the more peaceful occupation of hop picking in England. I ask Frenchey to oblige me with a song in German. He agrees conditionally, that I give one in French. Cries of "Horder for the good gentleman's song", and rattling thumps of approval with pots on the table are made. Frenchey sings the Watch on the Rhine, and I shout the Marseillaise.

The hoppers are astonished, and Frenchey is a greater hero than ever. I ask a young fellow near me why Frenchey excites so much interest. He tells me, "Well, look 'ere, he haint in his own country and don't know so much about things as we do; and if we was in his country we should like some one to help us, shouldn't we, sir?" I answer the feeling does the hoppers great credit, and am then further informed that Frenchey has just lost the whole of his tallies for his week's labour, amounting to some nine dozen bushels, and that they are about to make a subscription for him. My informant has already advanced him 1s 6d, a fact which he reminds Frenchey of by repeating every now and then, "Hi lent yon eighteen pence, didn't' I, Frenchey?" Frenchey acknowledges the indebtedness.

The beer is doing its work. Everybody is talking at the pitch of his voice but there are few listeners. Here is the true Hibernian ring, there the Cockney twang. We are all shouting.

Suddenly there comes another loud rattling of pots on the tables, and "Horder? Horder for a song", is called out from one corner. We have more songs, everyone sings. The music nor the words are not always the choicest, but the execution is in keeping with the general composition — Herin's love-ly 'ome, The dauntless faymale, The Convict of the Isle of France. One song finds especial favour, it bears the euphonious title of Johnny, I hardly knew yer, and has somewhat of the air of When Johnny comes marching home.

It is getting late. One or two over demonstrative ladies and gentlemen, full of beer and violence, have been bundled out by the landlord, and a fight or two has been got up outside. The landlord comes to tell us the party must break up.[4]

By the time of the First World War, the Bedford had become a much more orderly pub as this report from 1910 shows:

The Bedford Slate Club shared out on Monday evening when the following report was presented: 'In presenting our first annual balance sheet, we must congratulate ourselves on the good membership of the club. This being only the first year of its existence, it shows that a club of this kind has proved to be a long needed want at this part of town. We thank those gentlemen who are our hon. Members who have shown their appreciation of our work in such a practical manner. Although the sickness during the past year has been heavy the club remains sound. We have distributed to our sick members the sum of £21. 8s 4d and fulfilling the objects of the club namely to help one another in time of need. Seventy members each received a guinea, and seven half yearly members 10s 6d.[5]

During the Second World War the Bedford was run by landlady Daisy Blackman when Leslie Blackman was called up into the army. Daisy Blackman and the Bedford Arms made a significant contribution to the war effort as the unofficial rendezvous for the Rye Home Guard.

Jack and Marie Phillips   Telephone 3005

Bedford Arms

Across the road at the bottom of Landgate
THE MOST MODERN OLD PUB IN RYE

Snacks, Pies, etc.

ICED LAGER, FRUIT JUICES

Have your picnic   Ideal for children
and a glass of beer   Rear entrance on
on our lawn   Cricket Salts

1966

Romney Marsh was the front line for the Rye Home Guard as the threat of a German landing was a constant worry, and the local coastline provided many possible entry points. A pub story relates that the Germans landed a reconnaissance squad on Winchelsea Beach, and seized two members of the Rye Home Guard as prisoners of war. However, this story cannot be confirmed.

A second story, which can be confirmed, concerns the hop pickers during the Battle of Britain. Apparently, hop pickers took refuge in the Bedford after witnessing 'dog fights' overhead and being machine gunned in the hop fields.[6]

In 1946 the Bedford licence was transferred from Daisy Blackman to her husband Leslie when he was demobilised and had returned to Rye. After the war the Home Guard continued meeting in the Bedford well into the 1950s, as the 'A' Company Home Guard Old Comrades Association.[7]

Bedford Arms bar today

Borough Arms

Strand

c1900

So far little early history of the Borough Arms has come to light. What is definite is that by the end of the 16th century it was known by the sign of the 'Blue' or 'Blew Anchor', and was located near the original Strand Gate, demolished in about 1800.

The earliest reference to the Blew Anchor is 1592 when it was kept by a carpenter called John Hammond. A century later it was a well established licensed premises, and by 1728 it had become the London Trader, named after a type of coastal vessel then plying between the south coast ports and London. It was then Corporation property rented to Joseph Tucker at £3. 5s [£3.25] per annum.

From at least 1773 until 1853 the London Trader was paid 'allowances' by Rye Corporation – Chamberlain's vouchers – for the refreshment of men working locally.

A noted landlord was James Shearer (1838–1840). In 1875, many years after his time as landlord, the following article, a reference to the Scott's Float Sluice incident of 1830, appeared in the *South Eastern Advertiser*.

A BIT FROM LOCAL HISTORY

A centenarian died at Hamilton, near Glasgow, about a week since, a widow woman named Paterson, at the remarkable age of 105. She was a person of great vigour of intellect, and retained possession of all her faculties till within a few months of her death. Her descendants consist of 10 children, over 100 grand children 60 great grand children, and 2 great great grand children. In recording the above in our notice we must observe that the deceased old lady's maiden name was Shearer, and many of our readers in Tenterden, and a very great many more in Rye, will be able to call to mind a Mr James Shearer, a tailor, and father of Mrs Skinner Ranger of Tenterden, who died in this town about thirteen years ago, at the age of 87. The old lady above referred to was sister to Mr James Shearer. No doubt some old people of Rye will remember, after reading this notice, a rather wonderful episode in Mr James Shearer's life. We allude to the cutting of the new sluice, which took place about fifty years ago. Now it appears this somewhat interfered with the operations of the smuggling fraternity, who, with the assistance of a considerable mob of roughs and rioters, thought they could prevent the work from being carried out. A man of war had been sent down to Rye to protect the works, with orders to fire on the rioters should they persist in their unlawful measures. A large body of these misguided people, fully armed, were assembled in the back premises of the London Trader, at that time kept by Mr Shearer. As the time drew on, a conflict between the man of war's men and the rioters seemed inevitable. Mr Shearer addressed the latter from the 'Iron Bridge', pointing out the folly of their resistance to lawful authority, as also the likelihood of a great loss of life, and so prevailed on the men that they refrained from all further show of force. In connection with these events, Mr Shearer afterwards was one of the principal witnesses at the Assizes held at Kingston-on-Thames. – N.B. – Should any person in Rye be able to throw any further light on the affair, will he be kind enough to communicate to the editor.[1]

The editor's appeal elicited the following letter:

Sir, – In a paragraph from Tenterden, headed 'A Bit from Local History', in your last week's issue, you invite communications on the subject. I knew the late Mr James Shearer well. The episode in his life, there mentioned, cannot exactly be deemed 'Truth severe, by fairy fiction drest', although there is an amount of fiction in the account which mars the story. I do not remember at what date Mr Shearer kept the London Trader Inn; but that he was landlord of that hostelry then patronised by mariners. I can testify, and that the opponents of the New Scots-float Sluice, then in course of erection, might assemble in his back premises, I will not pretend to dispute, but that he did not address them from the 'Iron Bridge', as recorded, is obvious, because (as the comic song says) 'It wasn't built till after that'; it having been erected about 25 years, and the sluice nearer 50 years. Neither do I believe that smuggling had anything to do with the matter. About that time there was a 'Free Navigation Society' established in the town, composed of very respectable individuals, and it is most probable their meetings were held in the long back room of the London Trader. The neighbouring land owners and the members of this society were at issue, the former desiring a sluice to protect their land from inundation, and the latter anxious to secure a free course for the tidal waters as far inland as they would go, that at the ebb they might rush out and scour the harbour. The late Herbert Barrett Curteis, Esq., MP for East Sussex, as a land owner, engaged a few men-of-warsmen, stationed here to prevent smuggling, to protect the sluice from threatened injury, but no man-of-war was ever stationed here for protection to the sluice, and that gentleman being afterwards returned for the Borough of Rye, was a proof that no very hostile feelings existed between him and the inhabitants. These few remarks, entirely from memory, may elicit further information from some person better acquainted with the subject than myself.
    I am, sir, respectfully yours
    HENRY HEASMAN 1875 [2]

As one of the town's older inns the Borough Arms had more than its share of benefit societies. The Wellington Lodge of Freemasons was formed here in 1814. The Ancient Towns' Benefit Society, established here in 1828, was twice dissolved, the funds shared out,

Borough Tap and the Ship in the distance, 1890s

and then reformed. The society at that time had about 135 members, but by the 1860s it had transferred to the Cinque Ports Arms.

The Prince of Wales Odd Fellows was started here in 1842 with 115 members but later transferred to the Red Lion. The Foresters Harold Lodge was started here in 1855, also with 115 members, and also later transferred to the Red Lion.

The Unity Benefit Society was established here in 1859 with 35 members which by 1864 had increased to 80. They were still meeting here in 1881 when Unity Goose Raffles were a popular attraction. All of these clubs and societies, along with the 'opponents of the Scotts Float Sluice', used the 'long back' room on the first floor with an entrance in Trader's Passage. Other bars on the first floor included a 'sots hole'— a small curtained-off section for privacy. The corner building, now the Mermaid Corner Tea Rooms, was originally the tap room and later the public bar.

In the Great Depression of the 1890s beer consumption started to fall, and the London Trader found itself struggling to keep its custom. In 1893 the landlord, considering ways to improve his business, started selling greengroceries in the tap room, bringing complaints from the police. When he did this on a Sunday morning he was cautioned for trading 'during the hours of divine service', and obliged to stop.[3]

London Trader meat platter

His next innovation, in 1897, was to change the name from the London Trader to the Borough Arms. The brewers followed in 1901 with alterations and improvements. However, after 300 years the pub never regained its former vitality.

This was reflected in the fact that between 1900 and 1906 the Borough Arms had seven different landlords. One of them, Thomas Buckland, transferred from the London Stout House but stayed less than a year. None of the other six stayed more than a few months and the Borough Arms gradually lost favour.

Thus, in 1906 the police easily claimed that the pub had a history of falling demand, that it was redundant and 'no longer required'. After its closure the magistrate pointed out that the Ship, which he described as 'a superior house', was only 40 yards away, and that the trade of the Borough Arms had fallen to three barrels a week.[4]

A letter to the local paper signed by 'Onlooker' commented that:

There is only one public house which I would have voted for closing, and I have nothing to say against the brewer, the tenant, or the way in which the house is at present conducted. But I think of days gone by, when its victims have come out into the night air, and having been overcome, have stumbled to their doom.[5]

The writer was of course referring to the long flight of stone steps outside the Borough Arms and to an accident which had occurred there some time before!

Today, although no longer a public house, it is still known as the Old Borough Arms. This name refers to the old Strandgate, a few remains of which are incorporated into the Old Borough Arms itself.

In 1907 the Borough Arms was included in a property auction at the George, but the bidding reached only £190 and it was withdrawn.[6] The property then lapsed into a neglected state and later it was turned into housing, and the former corner bar into a customs office.

With the onset of the depression in the 1920s, the customs office became a Ministry of Labour Office attempting to find jobs on the quay and riverside.

drawing by Fred Roe c1900

Borough Arms plaque

Borough Arms today

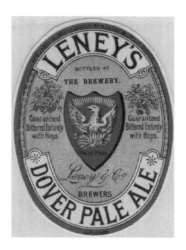

At the time of its closure the Borough Arms was tied to Leney's Brewery of Dover. Leney's Kentish Ales & Stout were famed the world over for their undoubted purity and were recommended by the medical newspapers of the time.

Leney's Dover Brewery

Bull Head
High Street

Buildings in Rye High Street, formerly Longer Street,
where the Bull Head was sited

The Bull Head or Bulls Head as it was also known, is mentioned in several early deeds and documents concerning property in Longer Street, now High Street, Rye.

It is first mentioned in 1690 at which time it was attached to a malthouse or brew house. It was then owned by Samuel Stretton, a clocksmith and town clerk of Rye in 1688.[1] By 1715 Samuel Stretton had leased the brewery to John Welch and the Bull Head to John Coleman, 'inn holder'.[2]

In 1724 the Bull Head and the brewery were both leased to John Welch. He insured the alehouse – 'known by the sign of the Bull Head in Longer Street' – for £200, and its contents for a further £300, with the Corporation of London Insurance Company for a premium of 16s [80p] per annum. In today's values, contents insurance to the value of £300 would be about £26,000, indicating perhaps that the Bull Head was furnished to a fairly comfortable standard. However, the insurance policy for the premises states that the building(s) was only insurable for about £17,000 (in today's terms), a small amount possibly because it was in disrepair.[3]

Six years later in 1730 the Bull Head is mentioned in the will of John Welch who was described as 'sick and weak in body but sound of mind and memory', and he left the 'messauge, tenement [property] and malthouse' to his son, also called John. The Bull Head was now occupied by William Barnes.

A Rye document of 1735 lists the licensed premises of Rye whose licensees had been fined that year. The document, titled: 'Fines on the Alehouse keepers of Rye, 1735', lists nine licensed premises including the Bulls Head whose landlord was then Richard Dawes. The name alehouse rather than inn is significant, and tells us that the Bulls Head did not have the status of an inn. The legal and technical definition of an inn was a licensed premises large enough to provide accommodation for travellers and their horses. In other words an inn must have letting bedrooms and stables. The reason for the fines and the amounts are not stated.[4]

More information is found in the Chamberlain's vouchers. The Chamberlain (borough treasurer) received income from local taxes, excise duties and rents, and paid the expenses of individuals who had served the Corporation in some way. These included jurors on court cases, members of Coroners Inquests, bell ringers and men who fired the guns at various celebrations. Men engaged in the repair of roads, streets, and buildings such as the church and the gaol, were accommodated in alehouses and paid for by the Corporation.

A Bill for the Sessions Dinner, at the Bull Head in Rye 4 Dec 1738.

Wine — — — — — — — —	5. —.
Beer — — — — — — —	. 4. –
Punch — — — — — — —	. 7. 6
34 Persons Eating at 1.6d each	2.11. –
7 Persons Eating at 1s each —	. 7. –
Servants — — — — — — —	. 5. –
	£8.14. 6

Pay to Mr Jewhurst the above Bill and this shall be your order, to be allowed in the Corporation Account.

This voucher suggests that the Bull Head kitchen and dining room were large enough to cater for this number of people.[5]

In 1752 the licence was held by Thomas Hovenden at the young age of 23, and in 1755 he is recorded as paying the local Poor Rate, 'an ability rate', of 6s [30p] to the Corporation in 1754. At this time the Bull Head was one of only seven inns and alehouses in the town. The others were the George, Lyon (or Red Lion), Dolphin, Fortune, London Trader and Two Brewers (which later became the Queens Head). The Bull Head's Poor Rate was set quite high being only one shilling [5p] less than the George, indicating a first class alehouse.[6]

Two years later in 1756, Thomas Hovenden gave up the Bull Head and took the licence of the George Inn, High Street where he was to remain for five years until 1761. After his removal to the George the Bull Head closed down and came to the end of its life as a licensed premises. This reduced the number of Rye inns and alehouses to six. No reason was given by Thomas Hovenden for the closure but it may have been because of a lack of accommodation for travellers.

However, in the same year, 1756, the premises were inherited by Needler Chamberlain Watson, a surgeon and member of the Stretton family. The Bull Head may have been closed by its new owner obliging Thomas Hovenden to move on, 'the house being intended by the landlord for his own private use'.

In 1756 John Welch Jnr raised some capital with a mortgage on the Bull Head, which mentioned 'two messauges and tenements, one of which is known by the sign of the Bull Head with yards, gardens, stables lately in the occupation of Thomas Hovenden, John Waters and William Payne ... and a malthouse lately occupied by John Hovenden', an unknown family member.

The Bull Head is mentioned in several sources as located in Longer Street – now High Street – but not precisely where in High Street. One source however, states the Bull Head was on the south side of the street adjoining the property of John Petter.

Having held the licence of the George for six years, Thomas Hovenden moved to the Swan, High Street, Hastings (1761–1777), and then to the Roebuck, Hastings (1777–1796). In the latter house he was described as a brewer.

THOMAS HOVENDEN, late of the **BULL HEAD** in Rye, Suffex, begs Leave to acquaint the Public, that he hath hired the **GEORGE** Inn in the faid Town, and is removed there. Whofoever will be fo kind as to favour him with their Cuftom may depend upon good Entertainment, and Stall Stabling for Horfes, and their Kindnefs fhall be gratefully acknowledged by
Their moft obedient humble Servant,

THOMAS HOVENDEN.

N.b. The Goods and Furniture of the faid Bull Head, are to be expofed to Sale on Wednefday the 27th Inftant, and continue till all are fold; the Houfe being intended by the Landlord for his own private Ufe. *

1756 [7]

* In this period the letter 's' appears to be written as 'f' except when a capital at the beginning of a word. All words that are stressed appear to start with a capital letter.

According to one source Hovenden had a reputation as a respected chef and baker in Rye, and people visited the Bull Head for his cuisine. In later years, after he had moved to Hastings, a certain amount of local custom went with him.

In 1769 Jeremiah Curteis, 'Inn holder', (then owner of the George, Red Lion and the London Trader) came to an agreement with Thomas Hovenden whereby he was 'released and discharged' of his financial responsibilities (in Rye).

Dunkling and Wright in their *Dictionary of Pub Names* speculate on the name Bull Head or Bulls Head. This old and common name, they say, may well have begun by referring to a papal bull, the lead seal attached to the pope's edicts (Latin 'bulla').

Another alternative theory applicable to a town with a protestant history such as Rye, is that a bull's head was an heraldic reference to the bull's head introduced into the arms of Henry VIII after he had defied the papal bull of 1538.

The term 'bull' also has one or two connections with drinking in certain colloquial expressions. In nautical slang, for example, a bull is, or was, a small keg of liquor. During the life of the Bull Head, Rye, a common nautical expression was to 'bull the cask or barrel'. This was done by pouring hot water into empty rum, gin and brandy casks, leaving it for a while before mixing and drinking.

Thomas Hovenden wearing a perewig

This was a common practice on the south coast. As late as 1854 for example, the Hastings coroner held an inquest into the death of a carter who died after drinking several measures of 'bull' from a 'bulled cask' at the Roebuck Inn, Hastings. The Roebuck landlord admitted at the Coroner's Inquest that it was a common practice to 'bull casks' for fishermen returning from a trip.[8]

It is quite likely therefore, that the malthouse or brew house attached to the Bull Head prepared and served 'bull' to the fishermen of Rye and others in the Bull Head tap.

Thomas Hovenden was the grandson of Thomas Hovenden (died 1727) and Elizabeth Hovenden (died 1753) both of Rye. He married Barbara Lidgold and they had four daughters. Thomas Hovenden died in 1797 aged 68 years. His body was returned to Rye from Hastings and he is buried in the north transept of Rye Church.

More buildings on the south side of Rye High Street, but which one was formerly the Bull Head?

Cinque Ports Arms
Cinque Ports Street

1930

The Cinque Ports Arms (1820–1943) should not be confused with the Cinque Ports (formerly the Railway), in the same street.

The Cinque Ports Arms was one of the most popular and widely used licensed premises in Rye. In its early years it was also known as a Post House and Excise Office, and for post chaise hire. Its first known landlord was Thomas Lancaster and the Excise Office supervisor was Jonathon Hodges.

1837 [1]

Sometime in the 1850s the Cinque Ports Arms expanded into the building on its eastern side, and in 1868 expanded again to accommodate a new assembly room. This increased the frontage of the premises to 141 feet [43 metres].

The Cinque Ports Arms was and remained a major venue for Rye's commercial classes, and throughout the 19th century many organisations and societies made it their headquarters.

The list of patrons is daunting but included: Rye Cricket Club, Rother Iron Works, Rye Bicycle Club, Rye District Commercial Association, Licensed Victuallers Association, Rye Choral Society, the Quadrille Invitation Society, Rye Harmonic Society, Rye Guardians, local farmers' 'Hop Dinners', friendly societies, gardening clubs and many others.

From 1862–1865 the local Rifle Volunteers had its headquarters here and the pub was used among others, as a billet for any military (particularly Inniskilling Dragoons) which might be passing through the town.

However, not all the customers were as welcome. The 'Lady Swindler' was a topic of conversation in the bars and parlour in 1875:

A LADY SWINDLER. — On Tuesday last, a rather handsomely-attired female, about 35 years of age, was driven by a Hastings flyman into Rye, and on her arrival she made inquiries at the Custom House for the French Consul, and produced some papers purporting to relate to some property belonging to her. Being informed the Collector had just left with the Superintendent of police, which was a rather singular coincidence, she took her departure, promising to call again, and in the meantime she drove to the Cinque Ports Arms and had some refreshment, not forgetting to entertain the driver, whom she afterwards prevailed upon to lend her 10s to enable her to make a few small purchases. She afterwards left the hotel alone, without paying the score, but stating that she should return to tea after transacting some business.

But instead of that she went to the Crown Inn, and hired a conveyance to take her to some friends at Winchelsea, stating that she was an invalid and unable to walk that distance, as she was one of the sufferers in the Shipton railway accident. On arriving at Winchelsea, she did not pay any visits, but directed the man in charge to drive to the railway station, as she was expecting some one by the next train. She then paid for the hire of the vehicle and dismissed the man, not forgetting to give him something for himself.

In the evening, the flyman began to get rather disconsolate at finding his fare did not return to the Cinque Ports Arms at the appointed time, and he instituted inquiries, calling at the Crown Inn, where he learned that a female answering the description had been taken to Winchelsea. After receiving this unwelcome intelligence he returned to Hastings, minus 10s. and his day's pay. The last tidings of the 'lady' were that she took a ticket at Winchelsea station for Ashford, and although the police have been put upon the qui vive, it is doubtful whether she will again visit this neighbourhood.[2]

A more welcome visitor arrived in 1879 when the Cinque Ports Arms was host to sporting celebrity Edward Weston. Weston was a long distance walker who held the world record for walking 500 miles in six days. The route of one of these 'Six Day Walks' included a section from Folkestone to Eastbourne, passing through Rye.

Weston had an entourage of other walkers, referees, journalists from *Bell's Life* (the sporting press of the day) and bookmakers representatives. The latter were busy checking and measuring times and distances because of the huge amount of gambling these events generated. The brief sojourn of this large crowd was spent in the Cinque Ports where they had breakfast, while locals placed their bets before the walk continued to Hastings, Pevensey and Eastbourne.[3]

Edward Weston, long distance walker 1879

In 1883 the Cinque Ports Arms was put up for auction. The pub then consisted of a bar, bar parlour, commercial and coffee room, smoking room, billiard room, mangle room, two sitting rooms and 13 bedrooms. There was also a kitchen, scullery, larder, pantry, beer cellar, two wine cellars, wash house, coal store, knife room, four coach houses, hay lofts, harness room, six-horse stable, five-stall stable, eight loose horse boxes, two four-roomed cottages, a large garden with summer house, chicken house, tool room, piggeries and a wood lodge.[4]

This large concern was let at an annual rent of £120. The rear of the premises adjoined the Cattle Market, and the principle thoroughfare for persons attending the market was through the hotel yard. This right of way was authorised by the Market Company for an annual payment of £1. 16s [£1.80p]. At the auction the Cinque Ports Arms was purchased by William Elliot of the Queens Head for £2,000.[5]

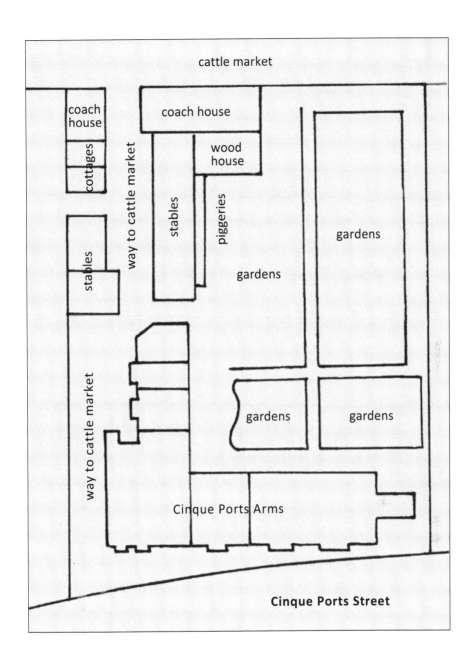

Cinque Ports Arms ground plan 1880s

1890

The life of the Cinque Ports Arms and the adjacent Regent Cinema came to a disastrous end when they were both bombed in 1942. Audrey Wright and William Burnham were the last licensees from 1940 to 1942. They then held the licence 'in suspension' for the brewery until 1946. In 1959 the county council purchased the site for £1,750 for the current Rye Police Station.

Cinque Ports Assembly Room
Cinque Ports Street

Cinque Ports Arms Assembly Room on right (with the two chimneys) c1910

The foundation stone for the Cinque Ports Assembly Room was laid in August 1868, and within three months it was open as an integral part of the Cinque Ports Arms. The Assembly Room, which was 50 by 25 feet [15.24m x 7.62m], extended the frontage of the pub to a total of 141 feet [43m], making it one of the largest licensed premises in Rye.

One user remembered the Assembly Room as an unattractive 'long, narrow shed like building'. For Rye's commercial and working classes at least, it quickly became a major entertainment venue and meeting place. For the next 60 years or so it was widely used by a large variety of groups and organisations.[1]

A list of those organisations who used both the pub and Assembly Room is endless but includes: the Rye Literary Debating and Elocution Society, the Quadrille Invitation Society, Rye Community Association, Orpheus Glee Union, Rye Cricket Club, Rye Suffragettes, Rye Liberal Association, Rye District Commercial Association and the YMCA Choir.

The venue, although licensed, was oddly enough acceptable to the Church of England Temperance Society who in 1905 gave presentations of 'lantern slides on the evils of alcohol' to audiences of up to 250. The Church of England Society for Providing Homes for Waifs and Strays also met here.[2]

Several theatre groups and companies put on pantomimes and stage plays over the years, but in 1899 pub landlord, John Reader, was charged for not having a theatre licence. The court decided that he had innocently broken the law, and would be fined 1s [5p] for each of the two days the theatre was open without a licence. The clerk suggested that "someone had been neglecting their duty because for 30 years plays have been performed here without a licence".[3]

In 1905 Ryers found themselves being photographed in the street:

A GREAT NOVELTY AT THE CINQUE PORTS ASSEMBLY ROOMS. — A highly interesting novelty is to be put forward by the management in connection with the programme at the Cinque Ports Assembly Rooms on Tuesday and Wednesday evenings next, February 28th and March 1st. For some days past operators have been busy with their cameras, taking snapshots 'here, there, and everywhere', as the saying goes, and dozens of residents have been taken unbeknown to themselves. On the evenings of Tuesday and

Wednesday next, these pictures will be placed in a box to be picked out by an independent member of the audience and then handed to the stage manager for the purpose of showing on a screen by a powerful lime-light bioscope. Should the originals of the pictures be in the hall they have only to step forward and claim the reward, in the shape of a handsome watch, walking - stick, or umbrella. Three pictures will be shown each evening, so that all the prizes are to be won. If your photograph does not come out on Tuesday it may on Wednesday. In addition to the above competition there is a splendid programme, including a drama in two scenes — a screaming farcical comedy and the wonderful 'Valan' in his entertainment of mystery, together with a number of other artistes of repute. In putting this entertainment before the Rye public it is hoped there will be a good attendance, and if well supported it will not be the last of such programmes whereby the public will benefit.[4]

By now the Cinque Ports Arms was tied to the Edwin Finn Brewery of Lydd, and in March 1913 they renamed the Assembly Room the Bijou Theatre, and applied for permission to make alterations allowing it to be used for cinematograph performances. The alterations also included installing electric light and updating the seating.

The Bijou Theatre opened on Easter Monday 1913 under the direction of Francis Bertram, whose stated aim was 'to provide the people of Rye with some highly refined hours of amusement'. The re-opening performance was described as 'a venture in vaudeville, presenting a combination of music, mirth and mystery and starring some novel and startling illusions, cabinet séances etc'.

BIJOU THEATRE. — It will be pleasing to the patrons of this theatre to know that the proprietor, Mr. Francis Bertram, will next week present, in addition to his usual attractive programme of picture novelties, a unique and charming Vaudeville attraction. The Four Happy-go-Lucky Girls will appear in a whirlwind of song and dance. They are direct from the London music halls. The pictures for the latter part of this week are being greatly appreciated, especially the story of "Dan Patterson, detective", which depicts some most remarkable and powerful plots and counterplots.
1913 [5]

BIJOU THEATRE,

RYE.

———

TUESDAY, NOVEMBER 9th

AT 3.0 and 7.30.

Jean Sterling MacKinlay

In Old Songs and Ballads, assisted by

HARCOURT WILLIAMS.

———

Popular Prices. Afternoon (Reserved), 3s.,
2s.;

Unreserved, 1s., Evening (Reserved), 2s.;

Unreserved, 1s., 6d., 3d., at Deacon's Library,
Rye.

1915

Bertram also promised that 'constant changes of programme will be the order of the day, intermittently combining vaudeville, drama and cinematography'. By this date the Bijou was also under the influence of the music hall, and indeed several performers who visited Rye came from that genre.[6]

By 1914, just after the outbreak of the First World War, the Bijou, now managed by John Hunter (formerly Entertainments Manager of Hastings Pier Pavilion), came to the attention of the police a second time. In December Hunter was charged with using the theatre to run a lottery. It was claimed 'that he did unlawfully sell certain tickets or chances not authorised by Parliament, to wit, a lottery for postal orders in an amusement house known as the Bijou Theatre'.

It was also claimed that: 'the case was of great importance because people were under the impression that this kind of lottery could legally be held. The programme, which sold for a penny, bore numbers, and at the conclusion of the concert Mr Hunter distributed money prizes to members of the audience who had programmes bearing certain numbers corresponding with those previously placed in an envelope. This we consider a very serious offence.'

Sergeant Sinclair of the Rye police said he went to the Bijou and paid 6d [2½p] admission. "The performance consisted of singing, dancing and pictures." At the end of the performance Mr Hunter stated from the platform that he had 15 prizes to distribute as a reward for patronage. After various witnesses were called, the magistrates considered that the case was proved, but said, "as there has been no similar charge before the Justices in Rye, we consider that Mr Hunter acted innocently and the case will be dismissed. But any further case will be severely dealt with."[7]

In 1915 during the First World War, Ellen Terry, then the leading Shakespearean actress in Britain, on a return visit gave four performances as Portia in *The Merchant of Venice*. She was supported by various well known actors including Jean Sterling Mackinlay, who also sang a selection of 'dramatic ballads and folk songs'.

These performances were a sell-out but were heightened by the attendance of invalid soldiers recently returned from the war in France and recuperating in the town. In the same year the Bijou was granted an extension 'for a Military Ball for Australian soldiers' billeted in Rye.

REGENT, RYE

'Phone 173.

RYE'S NEW AND MAGNIFICENT SUPER CINEMA.

| Continuous Nightly from 6 p.m. Mats. every Tues., Thurs. & Sat. at 2.30 p.m. | Western Electric SOUND SYSTEM | Prices (including tax); Balcony 2/- & 1/6; Stalls 1/6, 1/- & 7d. |

| MONDAY, DEC. 26th, for 3 Days only. Matinee Monday & Tuesday at 2.30:— | THURSDAY, DEC. 29th, for 3 Days. Matinee Saturday at 2.30:— |
| WINIFRED SHOTTER and OWEN NARES in THE LOVE CONTRACT *The merry escapades of a lady chauffeur.* | GRETA GARBO in AS YOU DESIRE ME GARBO'S GREATEST ACHIEVEMENT. |

LARGE FREE CAR PARK

1932

The magistrates decided wisely, that there will be 'no intoxicants, the bar will be closed and the rest of the premises shut off', showing that the Bijou was still part of the Cinque Ports Arms.[8]

From the 1920s screen shows increased in popularity, until eventually in 1932 the theatre was acquired and rebuilt by Shipham and King, proprietors of the Electric Palace, Landgate. It was reported that 'scenes of enthusiasm accompanied the opening of Rye's new luxurious cinema, the Regent. Long before the opening a large crowd had collected at the imposing modern building, illuminated by flood and neon lights. Rapidly every one of the 700 seats in the theatre was filled, and over 500 people were turned away. In the finely decorated vestibule were many telegrams congratulating Messrs Shipman and King on their enterprise.'

After the new cinema was formerly opened a speaker condemned the current vogue for gangster films. The first film shown was *Jacks the Boy* starring Jack Hulbert and Cecily Courtenage, supported by Laurel and Hardy and Mickey Mouse. This was followed by a Mayor's reception in the lounge.

In September 1942 the pub and the cinema were bombed and destroyed. The cinema however was rebuilt and reopened in 1948 and granted a six day licence. It was emphasised that the rebuilt

1948 [9]

cinema could not be used as a theatre as no safety curtain had been installed, and only a single stage exit was provided. The reopening film *My Brother Jonathan* starred Michael Dennison and Dulcie Gray.

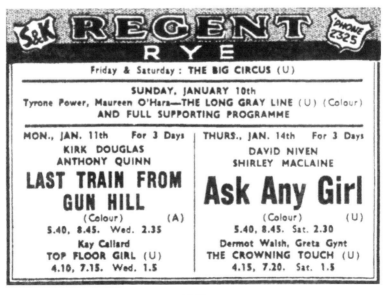

1960

REGENT

RYE
PHONE 2325
S&K

FRIDAY, SATURDAY — STEPTOE AND SON (A)

SUNDAY, JUNE 18 FOR 7 DAYS
RICHARD BURTON as Henry VIII
GENEVIEVE BUJOLD as Anne Boleyn

ANNE OF THE
THOUSAND DAYS

4.30, 7.45. Wed., Sat. 1.40   (A)

1972 [10]

The rebuilt cinema ran from 1948 until 1972, when it finally succumbed to the competition of television. In its final year the Regent, a cinema with 700 seats, attracted an average daily attendance of only 55! The final film was *Anne of the Thousand Days* shown on 18th June 1972. Thus the Regent outlasted the pub; the Cinque Ports Arms, to which it was once attached, by 30 years.

Regent cinema

Cinque Ports (Railway)
Cinque Ports Street

1925–1933

The current Cinque Ports public house first came into existence as the Horse and Groom sometime after 1834. In all probability it was a beer house before that date, but in any case it was fully licensed by 1838.

Its trade was boosted in 1851 with the opening of Rye Railway Station, and boosted again with the opening of the adjacent cattle market in 1859. However, there were constant complaints about the 'dreadful state' and condition of the road between the Horse and Groom and the railway station. At one point local residents and the landlord were obliged to carry out basic maintenance themselves.

From 1847 to 1857 Chamberlain's vouchers were issued by Rye Corporation for payment to the Horse and Groom, and for a period in the late 1860s vestry meetings were organised by the church in the club room.

At this time there was a widespread belief that alcohol had medicinal properties. Some even claimed that alcohol was 'good for you'. In 1867 when landlord Benjamin Heaver was charged with serving out of hours, he claimed he 'had only been serving brandy to a sick person'. A man had knocked on the door of the pub which was closed and said: "I am very poorly. Can you oblige me with a glass of brandy?" Heaver told the court that 'as a publican I am bound to serve the sick'. However, he was abruptly reminded that the law applied to everyone and was fined.[1]

A document which tells us a lot about the original Horse and Groom is a valuation of the furniture, fittings and stock drawn up in 1869, when the licence was transferred from William Norman to William Verrall.

The valuation shows that the old Horse and Groom was a sizable building with at least 15 rooms, including seven bedrooms, a club room on the first floor, tap room, bar, bar parlour, front parlour, kitchen, wash house and pantry. The Horse and Groom tap room was one of the most popular 'taps' in the town with a large custom from the market.

The 1869 valuation shows that the Horse and Groom carried a large stock including a 100 gallons of rum, gin and brandy!

6 gallons stout	2 gallons cherry brandy
23 gallons porter	½ gallon shrub
1 barrel ale	6 quarts ginger brandy
19 gallons other ale	½ gallon orange bitters
38 gallons cask rum	6 ½ quarts scotch whisky
30 gallons gin	15 ½ pints champagne
28 gallons brandy	ginger beer
9 bottles wine	1 quart other champagne
7 quarts peppermint	2 bottles cherry brandy

10 bottles Old Tom Gin	2 gallons cloves (cordial)
17 pints ale	4 quarts British brandy
6 quarts stout	3 ounces tobacco
9 bottles Hollands	1 box Havana cigars
cask vinegar	2 boxes other cigars
cask cider	quantity of clay pipes [2]

After the valuation the incoming landlord, William Verrall, changed the pub name to the Horse and Groom, Railway and Commercial Inn, a rather long name which was gradually shortened by use to the more simple Railway. However, it seems that until about 1875 both names: the Horse and Groom *and* the Railway were in use.

In 1885 the pub was demolished and completely rebuilt to become the premises that exist today. While demolition and rebuilding were in progress regulars were served in a cottage, one of several located behind the main building.[3]

It was unusual for the Rye magistrates to grant or allow a second additional licence for the same pub. Similar applications from other Rye pubs at different times, were nearly always turned down on the basis that this would increase the total number of licences in the town (see Ferry Boat Inn).

The newly built pub was immediately popular and gained a lot of new custom. In 1886 when Company 'E' – of the 1st Cinque Ports Rifle Volunteer Corps – was formed in the town, they chose the Railway as their watering hole. This was probably because their 'armoury' was established in the yard off the pub, and the agricultural hall in the market was initially used by the company's 60 volunteers as a drill hall.

The company's strength grew steadily until reaching a total of 115 Volunteers in 1906. The Railway remained their favourite port of call on drill nights, and the members of the Rye and District Rifle Club were probably influenced by the Volunteer custom to make the Railway their headquarters at the turn of the century. Another military connection was the fact that for many years the Railway was one of the pubs where Dragoons and other military were billeted when passing through the town.

At the beginning of the 20th century the Railway briefly became the headquarters of the Rye Bonfire Boys who held meetings and socials here. This may have been a different group from those who met in the Ypres Castle Inn.

The Rye Town Band was another group who patronised the Railway for social occasions but not for band practice. The pub 'smoker' was a popular way to spend a social evening before the First World War.

SMOKING CONCERT AT RYE
A VISITOR'S TRIBUTE TO THE TOWN

A private smoking concert was held on Saturday evening, at the Railway Hotel, Rye, on the occasion of the 43rd anniversary of Mr John Cocks' birthday. Mr. W. R. Ballard, the landlord, made a good chairman. He was supported in the vice-chair by Mr. D. Carey, and there were about 50 present, including a good number of the Rye Town Military Band. The following programme was carried out:

Opening selection,
    Zuy- der Zee, Rye Town Military Band;
    Violin solo, Mr. Gasson;
    Song, *Many Happy Returns,* Mr John Cocks;
    Cornet selection, *Birthday Wishes,* Bandmaster Bryan;
    Song, *The Lost Chord,* Mr Smith;
    Whistling solo, *The Blackbird,* Mr T Allen, *The Nightingale;*
    Song, *When the sun sets,* Mr G W Axell;
    Banjo solo, *Mr Playford;*
    Recitation, *'Pack of cards',* Mr J Cocks;
    Mandoline solo, *Black Bess,* Mr Sherwood;
    Song, *The Arab's Farewell,* Mr H S Carey;
    Violin selection: *Cavalleria Rusticana,* Mr Bartholomew;
    Song, *Queen of the Earth,* Mr Saxby.

Mr O Reeves accompanied the songs. Previous to the concert the band played several selections outside the pub under the able conductorship of Bandmaster Bryan. Mr John Cocks was called on for Many Happy Returns, and in reply, he said that he had taken a great liking for the old town and had greatly benefited in health by his stay in Rye. He was very pleased to make so many acquaintances, and he hoped to see them again next mackerel season. He would always recommend the lovely air and the fine fresh fish, and he greatly enjoyed the mackerel catching, as it was 'jolly good sport'. This was his fourth visit to the Ancient Town, and he hoped to have many more.

There were a number of friends from Rye, Rye Harbour, and Winchelsea present, and an enjoyable evening closed with the singing of Should Auld Acquaintance.

1907 4

In 1916, during the middle of the First World War, the Railway fell foul of the stringent restrictions of the military authorities. It was twice subject to a huge fine of £20 by the Liquor Control Board for supplying soldiers with bottled whisky. Hundreds of soldiers were billeted in Rye during the war including many convalescing from war wounds.

During the inter-war years the pub was host to the Railway Darts Club. Darts, then a relatively new game, was becoming more popular, and by 1925 the Railway was the base for the Ind Coop Darts Challenge Cup. Initially there were only four participating teams: the Railway, the George Tap, the William the Conqueror at Rye harbour and the Conservative Club.

From 1941 to 1946, two years after the outbreak of the Second World War, the licence was held by Gwendoline Muriel Marsden, a tenant of the George Beer and Rigden Brewery of Faversham. An inventory reveals that the Railway was still a large building of about 15 rooms including seven bedrooms. A look at the details of the pub contents is interesting.

All of the various earlier bars were now merged into three main rooms: the public bar, the saloon and the dining room. All of the toilets were accessed by 'penny in the slot locks', the bedrooms were furnished with 'mahogany commodes', framed pictures and marble clocks.

The dining room was furnished in mahogany and contained a 'Parisian striking timepiece in a marble case with a metal figure of Cupid'. Both bars had lino and coconut matting. There were railback chairs and bar stools in the public bar, and oak furniture in the saloon. Both were decorated with framed pictures: 'Hunting Scenes' in the saloon and 'Crinoline Difficulties' in the public bar. Fairly new items

THE RAILWAY HOTEL

CINQUE PORTS STREET - RYE 2319

Member of the Rye and District Hotels' and Caterers' Association

John and Mary McGrath

BED AND BREAKFAST

Hot and Cold Water, Electric Fires and Tea Makers
in all Bedrooms

Maryland Grill

Mary McGrath will specially prepare for you

SELECTED	TENDER	LOCAL
STEAKS	CHICKEN	FISH

12 noon to 1.30 p.m. and 7.30 p.m. to 10 p.m. (Sats. 9 p.m.)

1968

were cash registers, and among the glassware 'Pilsner Glasses' for the increasingly fashionable lager.

Both bars were equipped with 'pig's bristle dart boards' in cabinets and a new game for Rye, 'shove penny'. This game, not to be confused with 'shove halfpenny', had famously only been played in Hastings and Eastbourne for decades. This is the only known example of the game in Rye.

In 2008 a Hastings player reminisced to the author about the game. "Some players", he said, "cheated by keeping a chestnut in their pocket. Rubbing the nut and then the penny affected its performance, as the oil in the nut made the penny stick. Shovepenny boards were treated with paraffin, water or beer and cleaned with newspaper or a beer mat. Players prepared the pennies by heating one up and putting it onto a block of wood, which made a mould. A cold penny was put into the mould and smoothed with emery cloth or a surface grinder. This enabled players to have pennies of different weights, giving each coin its own characteristics. However, before matches all pennies were weighed."[5]

What else stands out in the inventory are the war time 'blackout curtains' and blinds made of paper. The signs: 'Railway Hotel Public Bar Entrance' and 'Railway Hotel Saloon Entrance' were decorated in red, black and gold leaf, and had their own 'blackout frames' to prevent any reflection at night.[6]

The name Railway continued until 1969 –1970 when it changed to the Cinque Ports, by which it is known today.

Cinque Ports today

Crown
Ferry Road

Crown 1970

The Crown opened its doors for the first time in about 1835. By 1839 it was fully licensed as the Crown and Sceptre, when the landlord was Edward Barnes.

Isaac Wright became landlord in 1859, and the Crown quickly became popular with those employed in the maritime occupations of the sea, the rivers, and the local shipyards. Mariners, boat builders, bargees, fishermen and sailors became the backbone of the Crown's custom. Indeed by the 1870s the pub was nicknamed the 'Sailor's Home'.

56

As with many Rye pubs the Crown has an association with smuggling. The Crown Yard was allegedly the site of a 'tub hole' for storing contraband. The tub hole 'was fitted with bevelled oak, and it was the duty of young Isaac to be let down into this hole to stack up the kegs as they were let down'. Isaac Wright and his sister 'with looks of supreme innocence', distributed these kegs in baskets covered with mangling around the Rye pubs!

The Crown Yard was also used by Wright's other business as a carrier. From here he completed weekly return trips to London with a six horse team. These were pre-railway days but after the railway station opened in 1851 the longer trips by horse drawn wagon ceased, and Isaac Wright became the local agent for the railway.

Within 20 years Wright had done well enough to purchase the Crown outright for £1,825 when it was auctioned at the George in 1879. He was also the tenant of the Crown Field which he rented from Rye Corporation for the low rate of £8 per annum.[1]

Isaac Wright was one of Rye's longest serving landlords. After his death in 1899 the Crown, the stables and a house behind were quickly auctioned at the George for £5,900.

Crown Yard was also the site of the Crown stables where post chaise, 'wagonettes' and various other modes of horse drawn vehicles were hired out. At least some of the people who worked here, the drivers, ostlers and stable boys, did so on a self employed or partially self-employed basis as the following court case in 1860 shows:

John Apps v. Isaac Wright. Claim for £4.10s [£4.50] for wages. Defendant is the well known carrier to the railway and landlord of the Crown Inn; plaintiff said he thought he was entitled to 7s [35p] per week besides the board and lodging. Defendant said Apps was amply remunerated by what he got from parties who frequented the house; he had stables which sometimes accommodated 40 horses in the course of a day; he fed plaintiff well and he had hay and water gratis; if he employed him with a fly or hearse he paid him for his services, which the plaintiff admitted. Plaintiff's son, who filled the office both before and after his father, corroborated defendant's statement. His Honour thought that plaintiff had been fully compensated for his services and found a verdict for the defendant.[2]

The land at the rear of the pub, formerly known as Crown Meadow, generated a large custom for the pub over the years. Crown Meadow was used by circuses, fairs, travelling theatres and indeed by anyone requiring a large open space. Some years, on Rye Gala Day, friendly societies dined in marquees on the Meadow. It was also used for playing the popular 19th century game of quoits. The Rye Branch of the Agricultural Workers Union was formed at an open-air meeting held on this ground, and other groups of trade unionists, including railway fettlers and platelayers, also held meetings here.

But not everyone was happy with the activities on the Crown Field. The following case went to court in 1881:

THE CROWN FIELD NUISANCES. Mr. Stephen Catt appeared before the Bench, and complained of the nuisance occasioned by a number of shows, a steam merry-go-round, &c., stationed in the Crown Field, and asked that something might be done to repel it. It was an unpleasant duty for him, but there were 12 or 13 caravans, and about 60 men, women, and children. From about half past six in the evening till past ten there was a continuous noise. On the day they came the whole of his place was beset with children. He was on very friendly terms with Mr. Wright, and did not object to circuses or shows being in the field, but for such affairs as these to be located there it was a great nuisance. It was like a fair, and, in fact, worse than the "Beggars' hill fair" used to be. And, as to sanitary arrangements, there were none, and they were, therefore, not acting in accordance with the requirements of the law on that point. He believed there were others in that neighbourhood who also objected to such proceedings, but he had come single-handed to tell his own tale. He would be the last person to stop any innocent amusement. This kind of thing, he was sorry to say, was of frequent occurrence. − His Worship said if there was a crowd the police ought to attend to it. − The Clerk (Mr. Walter Dawes) said the police must first request them to disperse if they were obstructing the roadway, and if they refused then they ought to be taken into custody, − Supt. Bourne said on the night the parties came to the town he saw the crowd at Mr. Catt's house and ordered them off. They were principally children; but he understood they assembled again when he left.[3]

However, not everyone agreed. Ten years later the local press commented: 'Whatever would become of Rye without the occasional shows that visit the Crown Inn Yard? Last Saturday night another one took up its position there, and roundabouting, shieing at cokers, shooting at bottles etc, went on apace. It is said that Englishmen love noise, and perhaps this is why the Crown Inn Yard possesses such an attraction for Ryers.'

In 1873 five crew members of a ketch [a two mast sailing boat] called the Guide, were brought into Rye by a local fishing smack [a fishing boat with a well for keeping fish alive]. The Guide was bound for Leith, Scotland with a load of apples but had accidentally been run down off the Norfolk coast by an Italian barque [a three mast sailing boat] called the Giovannino. The crew managed to get on board the barque but the cabin boy, who was rescued wearing only a shirt, was in a bad way. The crew had lost everything except what they stood up in. The Giovannino continued her voyage until she arrived at Rye Harbour where the shipwrecked crew were taken to Lloyd's Shipping Agents in Rye.

From there they were given hospitality by Mr and Mrs Wright at the Crown for which 'the poor fellows appeared exceedingly grateful'. Next morning, suitably re-clothed by Lloyds and nurtured at the Crown, the crew were soon on their way home via the train to London.

Another memorable Crown customer who turned up a year later was:

THE NOBLEMAN ORGAN GRINDER
This mysterious individual, about whom we have heard so much, since he first made his appearance in the southern counties, visited Rye on Monday last, and created no small amount of interest, as well as conjecture as to the truth of the story of his enterprise. Arriving in the town on Sunday, with his donkey and cart, it was his intention to make one of the principal establishments, which professes to provide "accommodation for man and beast", his head quarters, but, we understand, the worthy proprietor did not care to take in the organ grinder, illustrious as he is, therefore, he was compelled to seek shelter under the roof of the Crown Inn, where the hospitable host and hostess, Mr and Mrs Wright, entertained him in a manner which elicited his entire satisfaction. On Monday,

after going the round of the town, and replenishing the resources upon which it is stated, he and his donkey must live for three years, in accordance with the conditions of the wager, he took his departure in the afternoon en route for Tenterden, Ashford, Canterbury, &c. The Graphic of December 6th 1873, contains a faithful engraving of the noble grinder and his donkey and cart, surrounded by an admiring crowd, and refers to him as follows: − "Although the age of eccentric bets has almost passed away in this terribly dry, matter-of-fact, nineteenth century, and we no longer hear of gentlemen standing on London Bridge selling sovereigns for shillings, and other doughty wagers made after the third bottle of port, we now and then find an amusing instance of the love of human nature to out-do other people, be it in climbing up the

TO FAMILIES REMOVING.

ISAAC WRIGHT,

CROWN INN, RYE,

Is prepared to REMOVE every description of Furniture and Goods to all parts of the country on reasonable terms.   All orders have Mr. WRIGHT's personal attention, and the greatest care is exercised.

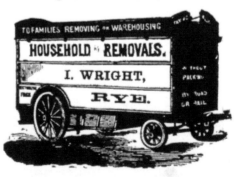

HEARSE AND MOURNING COACHES.

JOB MASTER.

ESTIMATES   GIVEN.

GOODS & FURNITURE CAREFULLY PACKED & REMOVED IN THE PANTECHNICON.

ALL KINDS OF FURNITURE, &c., WAREHOUSED.

AGENT BY APPOINTMENT TO THE SOUTH EASTERN RAILWAY COMPANY.

1888

topmost peak of an Alpine peak, or marching the length and breadth of a continent with a displayed standard. The last instance of the 'betting' mania comes from the sister isle, which for the past fourteen months has been in a fever of excitement concerning a certain amateur organ-grinder, who is confidently asserted to be a nobleman in disguise. He refuses his name to the curious, but owns to the fact that he is not what he seems, and has wagered to 'grind' his way through every province in the country."
1874 [4]

During the Second World War customers not called up were active on their allotments 'digging for victory'. The Crown by now had taken on the role of the Rye gardener's pub, promoting the production of locally grown vegetables and food, as a contribution to the war effort. Landlord Albert Pawsey set up and became secretary of the Rye Gardens and Allotments Association in 1940 after the Battle of Britain. The Crown was their headquarters throughout the war. Albert Pawsey retired in 1943 but the association continued for several years.

After the war, sometime between 1946 and 1947, the Crown became the headquarters of the Rye and District Trades Council, which started life in the Crown and held its monthly meetings there. It was also the meeting place of some of its affiliated Trade Union branches. The Trades Council represented their interests in the area.[5]

The Crown

Where you are assured of a warm welcome from Mr. and Mrs. Frank Rook

- FULLY LICENSED
- BED AND BREAKFAST
- REASONABLE TERMS

Charringtons Toby Ales

FERRY ROAD, RYE 3372

Member of the Rye and District Hotels' and Caterers' Association

---

c1960s

With a new Labour government after the war, and a new political atmosphere, the recent Rye Labour Party also held meetings at the Crown where, with the Trades Council, they campaigned on community issues and opposed evictions of tenants by the County Council. The presence of both organisations continued well into the 1950s and beyond.

Crown today

Dial
101 High Street

101 High Street, formerly the Dial, today

The most noted landlord of this public house was Stephen Gilbert Fryman. He first came to light in 1824 when he purchased the Bridge Inn, Winchelsea for £60, and sold it two years later for £116 making a handsome profit. But whether he held the licence as well as being the owner, is unknown.

Bridge Inn, Winchelsea today

What is known is that around 1826 Stephen Gilbert Fryman, was half of a trading partnership under the name of Fryman and Watts, Wholesale Grocers and Tallow Chandlers, Market Street. This business was still listed in Piggot's Directory for 1840.

At some point he acquired the premises at 101 High Street, which from the late 17th century to the late 18th century had been in the occupation of the Gill family of clockmakers.

Today Rye lays claim to two 'Parliamentary Clocks', one in the Town Hall and the other in the George. Both these clocks were probably made and supplied by the Gill Family although they are unstamped.

As a response to the Clock Tax of 1797 which increased the price of clocks and watches, many public clocks were erected on both private and public buildings. As you might expect from a clock designed to be publicly displayed, they were often large and solidly built. The Gill family had their own clock mounted on the front of their premises in the High Street advertising their business. However, it was not strictly a Parliamentary clock as the Gills had stopped making them before the tax was introduced.

Sometime around 1820 the premises became a public house known as the Black Boy and Still, and later as the Dial or Dial House, obviously indicating the public clock on the front of the building.

Various deeds list some of the occupants and possibly owners of the Dial, but not always the dates of their occupation. A conveyance of 1854 states that 'it was at one time occupied by Thomas Earl, since of William Payne, since of Sarah Barnes, since of Charles Pilcher, since of Edward Hilder, since of Thomas Bourne, since of Henry Bourne and now of Stephen Gilbert Fryman'. Henry Bourne by coincidence also a clockmaker, applied for a full licence in 1831, and again successfully in 1832.[1]

The deed also tells us that in 1848 Stephen Gilbert Fryman was declared bankrupt. Bankruptcy papers lodged in the National Archive state that his property included the 'said messuage or tenement which was formerly, and again recently licensed as, a public house … was heretofore called or known by the name of the Black Boy and Still, but is now called or known by the name of the Dial'.[2]

Thus it seems that the premises was licensed before 1830. The licence then lapsed, was restarted by Henry Bourne in 1832, and continued by Stephen Gilbert Fryman into the 1840s.

Stephen Gilbert Fryman's bankruptcy is also listed and reported in the *London Gazette* for 1849, where he was described as a Wine and Spirit Merchant, Dealer and Chapman (ie pedlar or merchant). The Dial is not mentioned.[3]

After his bankruptcy in 1848 the Dial was sold by his assignees as a public house. A further document states that the assignees of 'Stephen Gilbert Fryman a bankrupt, sold the public house known as the Dial in Longer Street (now the High Street) to James Jenner, Gent of Portman Square, London for £495', in 1854.[4]

However bankruptcy only stopped him from trading for a short period of probably 12 months. By 1850 he was trading vigorously as a wine and spirit merchant, and in the House of Commons Enquiry into corrupt practices during the Rye election of 1852, Stephen Gilbert Fryman is listed as the major supplier of wines and spirits to the numerous Rye public houses and eating houses, who gave out free food and drink during the 'treating scandal' of that general election.

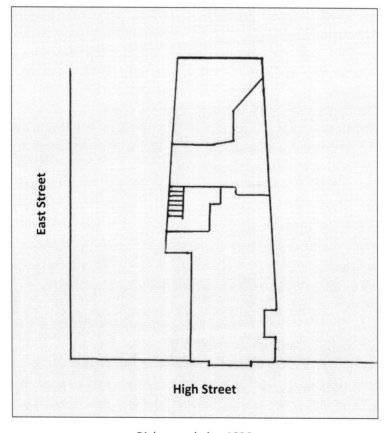

Dial ground plan 1886

At a property auction held at the George Inn six years later in 1858, Fryman, still trading as a wine and spirit merchant, purchased another property (now part of the museum) and land in East Street behind the Dial, for £165 from Eliza Turner, spinster of Bexhill. In 1863 and again in 1864 the Dial is listed and named as a fully licensed public house in the annual reports of the Rye Brewster Sessions. Unfortunately the licensee is not named.[5]

Then in 1874, 25 years after his bankruptcy, Fryman re-purchased the former Dial from the executors of James Jenner, one of whom was himself, for £520. This action suggests that he greatly resented being made bankrupt and losing the former Dial public house to his creditors, and was determined one day to regain its ownership.[6]

Finally in 1875 a mortgage describes the premises as: 'kept for many years as a public house known as the Black Boy and Still, now

---

HERBERT V. CHAPMAN

(Late CRAMP & FRYMAN),

WINE & SPIRIT MERCHANT,

101, HIGH ST., RYE, & POPLAR HOUSE, LYDD

CLARETS ...   ...   15/-, 18/-, 21/-, 24/- and 30/- per dozen.

VERY FINE ST. ESTEPHE, bottled in 1881 ... 36/-   "

SPECIALLY SELECTED VINTAGE CLARETS AT MARKET PRICES.

BOTTLED ALES ... ...   2/6 and 3/- per dozen, Imperial pints.

COMBE & CO.'S BOTTLED STOUTS 2/6 AND 3/- per dozen.
                                                                  Imperial pints.

BASS & GUINNESS ... ...   4/- per dozen, Imperial pints.

SPECIAL BLENDS IN IRISH & SCOTCH WHISKEYS.

FRESH YEAST FROM THE BREWERY DAILY.

1888

the Dial, many years in the tenure of Stephen Fryman'. This is the last reference to the property as a fully licensed premises. As far as is known it was never again in use as a public house, and by 1878 the premises were in the hands of his son Egbert Fryman.[7]

In 1886 Stephen Gilbert Fryman, now described as 'Gent of Chiswick', sold the premises to John H E Cramp of Rye for £1,100, who then leased the property to Herbert Verral Chapman, brewer of East Guildford (later Chapman Bros). At that time Chapman owned or leased six licensed houses in Rye, including the Globe, Greyhound, Tower, Ferry Boat and London Stout House. Stephen Gilbert Fryman died in 1894 leaving his wife Jane and his son Egbert to manage his interests. In 1901 the land at the rear of 101 High Street was conveyed to Chapman Bros, after it had been sold by Egbert Fryman for £400 in 1895.

Egbert Fryman was then an employee, or perhaps a partner of Chapman Bros and was, in 1899, instrumental in the rebuilding of the Ferry Boat Inn, Ferry Road, and in that pub's reopening in 1900 as the New Inn. He also had a major role in overseeing and promoting the revamped London Stout House during those years. He was known to be quite vocal in opposition to the Rye temperance movement.

By 1900 the former Dial public house had become a part of Chapman Bros wholesale storage and distribution network and an off-licence. In 1920 it was conveyed from Chapman Bros to Edwin Flynn, Brewers of Lydd, who eventually became part of the Style and Winch Brewery of Maidstone.

According to the *Dictionary of Pub Names*, in the 18th century the name 'Black Boy' was a common name for taverns and coffee houses, and was usually a reference to a personal servant of a rich person. By the 19th century it was more likely to portray a young chimney sweep. A 'still' is the apparatus at the centre of the distilling process by which alcohol is produced.

Eileen Bennett in *Rye Memories* recalled that she 'was secretary to the author Radcliffe Hall at the Mermaid Inn, and later ... at 4 High Street, which she [Radcliffe Hall] named the Black Boy after Charles II, because of his dark skin'.[8] However, although having a similar name, 4 High Street should not be confused with the former Dial at 101 High Street.

It is tempting to speculate that die hard Royalists drank here and secretly toasted 'the blackboy over the water' during the Protectorate (1653–1659).

The name Black Boy most probably originated with a former tenant who was a Royalist and a supporter of Charles II. Apart from the connection with Charles II, there is also the possibility that the name referred to a black mooring buoy located in Rye harbour — but this is only speculation.

By the 1960s the premises were in the hands of Carlos and Thrale Ltd, described as 'hirers of cocktail bars and equipment for parties'. The building is now the Rye Age UK shop.

CARLOS & THRALE Ltd.

The Wine and Spirit Merchants of the district, who can loan you absolutely **free of charge**

COCKTAIL BAR

Cocktail Shaker, All Types of Glasses, Water Jugs, Bottle Openers, Serviettes, Drip Mats and a Punch Bowl

Prompt Deliveries in Town and District

101 HIGH STREET, RYE

Phone Rye 3304

OUR SHOP IS AS NEAR AS YOUR NEAREST
TELEPHONE

1960s

Dolphin
Gun Garden

The above photograph shows the attractive site of the Dolphin alehouse, formerly situated in the open space opposite Ypres Castle on or near the Gun Garden, Rye from 1710 until 1801. As of yet no known drawing or sketch of the Dolphin has come to light and we are only informed by brief references to it.

The dates and names of Dolphin landlords and landladies are almost totally provided by information included on Chamberlain's

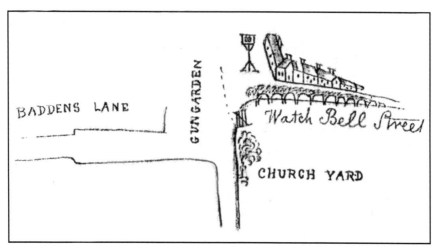

An early map of 1771 showing the sign of the Dolphin

vouchers issued to the alehouse by Rye Corporation from 1710. In that year landlord Bethyer Hayden was granted the sum of 1s 6d [7½p] for refreshments for 'the men that fired the guns' at a celebration in the Gun Garden, and in the same year 3s 4d [17p] 'for beer for the ringers'.[1]

Another licensee George Ogley, landlord from 1739 to 1740, was granted payment via Chamberlain's vouchers 'for the bricklayers who drank at the above house when at work upon the gaol' ie when repairing the Ypres Castle tower opposite, then in use as the town gaol.[2]

Many later voucher payments were 'signed' for by landlady Ann Bean (widow 1753–1766) who was obviously illiterate and simply put an X against her name. The X was then witnessed by someone else as 'her mark'. After the 1770s the Dolphin alehouse seems to have fallen out of favour with the Corporation and the issuing of Corporation vouchers went into abeyance.

Another local document referring to the building which was formerly the Dolphin, takes us forward into the following century long after the Dolphin had closed. This document is an order made by the Rye Poor Law Commissioners in 1837 for the purchase of land and property in the Gun Garden.[3] The land was required for the alteration and extension of the Union Workhouse, and the order was for the purchase of all property and gardens situated and adjoining the west side of the Union Workhouse in Watchbell Street, mainly occupied by George French. Soon after, George French became the licensee of the Ypres Castle Inn on Gun Garden steps opposite.

A second document, also from 1837, records that the above purchase took place. The purchase was of: 'all that property *formerly* known by the sign of the Dolphin and the stables, buildings, gardens ... on or near the Gun Garden or old churchyard. It also included adjoining property 'chambers, gardens and premises' belonging to Stephen Gilbert Fryman.[4]

Both documents detail, what was by then, the *former* Dolphin 36 years after its closure as an alehouse. This is an important point as some local authors have previously misinterpreted the existence of this building *as the* Dolphin alehouse and not as the building which was *formerly* the Dolphin alehouse. At least one local author has quoted the building of the extension of Rye Union Workhouse in 1837 as the reason for the closure of the Dolphin Alehouse, and other authors have unfortunately followed suit. However, this was not the case. The Dolphin closed for reasons unknown in 1801. The workhouse was extended in 1837.

The Dolphin is said to be named after a ship of the same name— a privateer of 35 tons usually at berth in Rye Harbour. Thomas Pierce, mariner of Rye, was the master in the 1740s and a customer of the Dolphin alehouse.

However the *Dictionary of Pub Names* by Dunkling and Wright informs us that the name Dolphin is a common one for public houses by the sea. The name comes from a seafaring, Neptunian legend; a piece of fishing mythology which states that in days gone by dolphins were thought of as fishermen friendly animals. It was commonly believed that they wound themselves around a boat's anchor cable thus stopping the cable from dragging, and giving the boat extra stability.

The Dolphin alehouse formerly of the Gun Garden, should not be confused with another, second licensed premises also called the Dolphin located in the Mint from 1826 to 1865. In the latter year this licensed premises changed its name to become the Foresters Arms.

In 1710 landlord Bethyer Hayden was granted the sum of 1s 6d [7½ p] for refreshment 'for the men that fired the guns' at various celebrations in the Gun Garden!

A German traveller in England once noted: 'The English are vastly fond of noises that fill the air such as the firing of canon, beating of drums and ringing of bells, so that it is common for a number of them to go up into some belfry and ring bells for hours together for the sake of exercise.'

Ferry Boat Inn
Ferry Road

1838–1898

The Ferry Boat Inn shown here should not be confused with other Rye pubs and ale houses of the same or similar names at earlier dates. For example, a Rye document with the title: *'Fines set by the Mayor on Alehouse Keepers 1722'*, lists John Noble at the Ferry, and also John Beeching at the Ferry House.[1]

A second document 12 years later in 1735 called: *'Fines on the Alehouse Keepers of Rye 1735'*, lists William Curtis as landlord of the Ferry. But there is no mention of the Ferry House. Thus we have two different licensed premises known as the Ferry and the Ferry House.[2]

The earliest known deed for a pub called the Ferry Boat is dated 1709. This document is a lease between Rye Corporation and a local carpenter called Edward Dodge, for land on which he subsequently built a dwelling house and stables.

In 1760 the remaining portion of the same lease was transferred to Dr Thomas Frewen of Rye, who immediately transferred it to John Stoneham of Beckley, yeoman.[3] In 1782 Henry Stoneham of Brede, sold rights in the Rye Ferry/Strand Ferry, which presumably included adjoining property, to Jeremiah Curteis of Rye. John Stoneham (number two), a son, did the same in 1801. The important clue here is 'Strand Ferry', which presumably was another ferry, crossing the Tillingham from the Strand, with accompanying buildings and an alehouse and therefore another Ferry Boat Inn.

Back at Ferry Road meanwhile, in 1832 executor Edward Curteis 'sold the tenement (now in three dwellings), together with a further four dwellings where the stables had been built to James Smith, builder of Rye'. The property then passed to his son Jeremiah Smith (Rye's infamous Mayor), who assigned it in 1843 to Richard Curteis Pomfret of Rye. It is assumed that the above property and the 'further four dwellings' had now become the Ferry Boat Inn public house.

James Glasier is listed as landlord in 1852 when the Ferry Boat received funding for free food and drink in the 'treating scandal', during the General Election of that year. A lease of 1867 lists 'the Ferry Boat Inn with adjacent cottage occupied by a Mrs Chapman'. Could she have been related to Chapman's brewery?[4]

In 1865 the Ferry Boat came into the news when a young woman was charged for stealing a man's cap whilst he was playing dominoes.

Other customers in the same games room were playing 'Kick up Jenny', a game of which the magistrate had never heard. At the magistrate's request the game was described to the court by one of the players as 'a miniature kind of nine pins where instead of throwing a ball at the pins or skittles you swing a lead ball suspended from the ceiling on a thin rope'. The court was assured that 'Kick up Jenny' was a game of skill and not a form of gambling.[5]

According to the English Heritage publication *Played at the Pub,* a very similar game, or perhaps the same game, known as 'Devil Among the Tailors', was common in other parts of the country at this time. A small wooden ball, the 'devil', was tethered by a light chain or cord to a swivel at the top of a pole. The ball was thrown by the player around the pole to clatter among the nine small pins, known as the 'tailors', which were set up in a diamond formation. Kick up Jenny seems to have been the Rye version.

'Devil Among the Tailors'

In June 1866 the four adjoining cottages and the Ferry Boat Inn were sold for £500 to the East Guildford Brewery. The Ferry Boat Inn was to remain tied to the East Guildford Brewery, later Chapman Brothers Ltd, and later Courage Ltd, for the remainder of its pub life. The semi-rural setting of the Ferry Boat was revealed in a police report of 1870. A constable attempting to approach the pub undetected, walked in from the open fields behind!

THE NEW INN

FERRY ROAD, RYE

(LATE THE FERRY BOAT),

HAVING BEEN ENTIRELY RE-BUILT IS NOW OPEN TO THE PUBLIC
under new Management

Good Accommodation,

Ales, Wines and Spirits of the Best Quality.

Proprietor:-

JAS. WM. JENNINGS

Late of the Railway Inn,

Eridge.

1899

In 1898 an application was made by Egbert Fryman (son of Stephen Gilbert Fryman — see the Dial), agent for the brewers, for permission to demolish and rebuild the Ferry Boat Inn:

Mr E. Fryman, applied on behalf of Messrs Chapman Brothers, for leave to serve customers in the lower room of the cottage adjoining the Ferry Boat Inn while the house was being built. The Mayor thought that this would amount to the granting of a licence for a fresh house and it was adjourned.[6]

Unlike a similar request made and granted in 1885 when the Cinque Ports/Railway pub was rebuilt, the licensing magistrates were by now under the pressure of the temperance lobby, and very careful not to increase the total number of licences in the town.

The following year, 1899, Egbert Fryman applied again. But this time to change the name from the Ferry Boat Inn to the New Inn, a name which by the 1890s had become fashionable as a pub name. The magistrates agreed the change but said they were 'sorry to see the old name go', because they felt the name Ferry Boat Inn was closely identified with the community.[7]

Two months later Egbert Fryman presided over the opening celebrations of the New Inn which was 'new' in all senses: a new building, a new name and a new landlord!

Almost immediately the New Inn became one of Rye's most popular and successful licensed premises. In 1900 the New Inn Slate Club, 'the first and only slate club in Rye', was set up by two regular customers, Edwin Twort, a pottery worker and Richard Halliwell, who became club chairman and secretary respectively. Twort was employed at the local Bell Vue Pottery, and other potters were soon to be found patronising the New Inn bar and among the membership of the slate club.

From 1900 until the outbreak of war in 1914 the New Inn Slate Club was incredibly successful, gaining 300 members in its first six years. Apart from annual 'share-outs' and sickness payments, members also enjoyed social evenings together at 'Smoking Concerts' known as 'smokers'.

The 'harmony' or singing at these concerts was so highly regarded that the pub was always packed for these events. Quite

New Inn c1905

often local residents who couldn't get into the pub would gather in the road outside to listen to the 'harmony'.

Edwin Twort's death in 1912 and the coming of the First World War brought to an end a very busy period in the history of the New Inn. The slate club however, continued for many more years.

Adams Guide to Rye, 1934, mentions the former Ferry Boat Inn on the 'site of the ferry to Cadborough'.[8] The pub kept the name New Inn for some 60 years, until in the early 1960s it reverted back to its former name of the Ferry Boat Inn. An historic photograph of the street was published in 1970 with the comment: 'now the Ferry Boat'.[9]

However, at some point in the 1960s it appears to have been closed and is not listed in the telephone directory for several years until, in the mid 1970s it reappeared, yet again, as the Ferry Boat Inn. Since 1991 this former public house has been a private residence.

c1960

Ferry Boat today

Flushing Inn
Market Street

The Flushing Inn where Breads the murderer was taken for a 'last drink' in 1743

In 1729 Rye butcher John Breads became owner of the property known as the Flushing Inn, and opened a slaughter house in the rear yard. There was nothing unusual about this as Market Street, then known as the Butchery, was the location of the town's butchers. In 1739 Breads let the house to John Igglesden who opened it under licence, and presumably gave the inn its unusual name. Igglesden may have simply named the Inn after the Dutch town of Flushing (Vlissingen to the Dutch), or because of his own privateering excursions across the English Channel.

Four years later in 1743 John Breads became the assassin in Rye's most famous murder case, when he mistakenly stabbed ex-mayor Allen Grebbell to death in Rye churchyard, thinking he was the mayor, James Lamb. The most common version of this story relates that Breads had fallen out with Mayor James Lamb, who had previously fined him for selling meat under weight.

On a dark night in March 1743, Allen Grebbell was returning home after attending a party aboard a revenue cutter moored near the Fish Market. He was wearing a red cloak borrowed from the mayor, as it looked like rain. He made his way through Rye churchyard where Breads lay in wait, and at a certain spot Breads leapt out from behind a gravestone and stabbed him twice in the back. Because of the mayor's red cloak he had mistaken Grebbell for Lamb and had murdered the wrong man.

A few hours into the early morning Breads was apprehended in the town as he staggered around drunk shouting "butchers should kill lambs", and was arrested. The bloodstained, bone handled knife used on his victim was later retrieved from the churchyard.

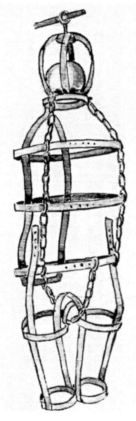

The skull of John Breads

After his arrest Breads was tried in a warehouse on the Strand by the very person, James Lamb, he had intended to kill. After being found guilty he was incarcerated in the Ypres Castle tower, then in use as the town gaol, and was to remain there for many months. On his way from the gaol to the gibbet he was taken into the Flushing Inn, which he still owned, 'for a last drink' before being hung on Gibbets Marsh. His body remained on the marsh for 50 years withering away. This gruesome legend relates that old women removed parts of his flesh as a cure for rheumatism! The skull of John Breads, which is all that remains, can be seen today in Rye Town Hall.

Under Rye's ancient laws, his property became forfeited to the corporation upon his conviction and execution. However, out of compassion to his fatherless children, the corporation took over his property including the Flushing Inn, and administered it for his children's benefit until the youngest reached the age of 21 years.

In the meantime John Igglesden remained licensee of the Flushing Inn until 1750. He was succeeded by William Marchant who failed to make a success of the inn, and gave it up in 1752. He was apparently unable to pay his rates, and the collector wrote 'broke' against his name.

By 1756 Joseph and Richard Breads, the two surviving sons and, under the law of Kentish Gavelkind, the heirs of John Breads, became of age and inherited the Flushing Inn which, with the slaughter house in the yard, they immediately sold off. One of the sons, Richard, later became landlord of the Queen's Head in Landgate.

The Flushing Inn is also noted for a 16th century fresco painted on one of its internal walls, and discovered in 1905. The discovery was reported at the time in the local press:-

THE OLD FLUSHING INN
INTERESTING DISCOVERIES AT RYE

Our readers will doubtless recollect that a few weeks ago we drew attention to the discovery of certain antique oak pannelling during the progress of alterations to a dwelling-house in Market-street. At that time there were numerous indications that the property dated back a good number of years, and a further and more interesting recent discovery unquestionably confirms the fact.

Messrs C Fletcher and Son have been engaged on the work of renovation for some time past, and on Monday morning, whilst Mr E G Fletcher was sounding a partition or wall, which proved to be of oak pannelling, a small piece of plaster fell away, which, upon examination, was found to have an old English letter on the back. The pannelling was removed, and behind it was found a fresco, old English in character, clearly displayed on the plaster.

The subject of the fresco is allegorical, but so clearly portrayed that a student of mythology would experience little difficulty in comprehending its portent.

The figures depicted remind one of some of the beings to be met with in the Inferno of Dante, though evident attempts have been made to figure gentler denizens of either creation or imagination in addition. The general idea of the fresco suggests a scriptural origin, for it bears the Latin text, "Soli Deo Honore" (to the honour of God only) thrice transversely. Also, towards the top of the fresco,

A section of the painted fresco

is inscribed the *Magnificat*. It is divided into three sections, and a part appears on each in the form of a scroll, supported by tiny nymphs. Only the first inscription is legible, the other two having been broken during the course of time. Old English lettering is employed, and also the original version of the *Magnificat*, running something as follows:- "My soul, it doeth magnify ye Lord and rejoyce in its God. He hath seen and regardeth his lowly handmaydn. All generations call him blessyd. He that is mighty hath done to me great things, and blessed is His name."

The fresco occupies the whole of the one side of the room, and though in places it has become defaced and broken, it is certainly in a remarkable state of preservation, considering its age. There is a coat of arms in the left-hand corner bearing lions rampant, and the fleur-de-lys, but its origin cannot be traced, as only a part is visible. Altogether, the fresco is a wonderful example of an ancient master's skill. Its future has not yet been decided, a question that will be awaited with interest.

The panelling taken from the walls is also worthy of note. It is richly carved, and certainly dates back some centuries. The cellars, too, are well deserving of inspection. They are capacious and overlapped with fine arches, and commodious enough to suit the purposes of the old freetraders ("smugglers" in this case), who did an extensive but illicit trade with the merchants of Flushing years ago.[2]

The Flushing Inn
Market St., Rye

Telephone
Rye 3207

A 15th Century

HOTEL and RESTAURANT

that has been growing old gracefully
for more than six centuries

WITH   MODERN   HOTEL   AMENITIES—
FINE   FARE   AND   COURTEOUS   SERVICE

Brochure and Tariff on application

Proprietors: Mr. & Mrs. A. J. Mann, M.H.C.I.

**HISTORICALLY RENOWNED 16th CENTURY FRESCO AND
ANCIENT EARLY ENGLISH CELLAR, 11th Cent. (circa)**

Member of the Rye and District Hotels' and Caterers' Association

c1950s

The Flushing Inn is thought to have been used by smugglers as its rear courtyard stretched to the edge of a cliff, where contraband could be hauled up and delivered into the Flushing cellars. It is commonly believed that the Inn's name is derived from the illicit trade between Rye and the Dutch port of Flushing in the 18th century. Another theory as to the origin of the name includes the fact that Market Street was the location of the town's butchers and was previously known as the Butchery. An early name for a butcher was 'flesher' and over time Flesher's Inn might have become corrupted to Flushing Inn. However, as the Flushing Inn was only initially licensed for 13 years, this seems unlikely.

In 1960, after 208 years, the Flushing Inn was re-licensed as an hotel and restaurant. It remained licensed for 50 years until 2010, after which time it became once more a private house.

Flushing Inn c1960s

Forester's Arms
Mint

Forester's Arms with suspended lamp

The Forester's Arms started life as the Dolphin Inn in the mid-1820s. It is listed in the 1826 street directory when the landlord was Richard Heath. In later years the pub became one of a trio of public houses on this part of the Mint, the other two being the Swan and the Standard Inn.

Customers using the bar parlour included jurors who had been summoned to attend Coroner's Inquests. Two early landlords: Edward Edwards (1854) and Thomas Shearer (1856) were both requested by Rye Corporation to provide sustenance to members of Coroner's Inquests. Thomas Shearer for example, was asked in 1856 to provide 'thirteen jurymen with refreshment of one shilling each' [5p]. The inquests did not take place in the pub, but elsewhere.

> Mr Thos. Shearer Dolphin Inn
> 29 Nov 1856.
>
> Thirteen jurymen to have refreshment to the extent of one shilling each.
>
> £0 13 -0   Edwin Nath James
> 1857 Jay 30

1

A valuation of the property carried out in 1853 listed the fixtures and furniture in the premises, and shows the building to be quite spacious indicating that the Forester's was created from two adjacent properties. In 1853 it had three 'attick' (sic) bedrooms on the second floor and four other bedrooms on the first floor. With an unused room and a clubroom this made a total of nine rooms on the first and 'attick' floors. On the ground floor there were two bar parlours, a bar, taproom, kitchen and washhouse.

As per usual the taproom was minimally furnished with deal benches fixed to the floor and deal tables standing on an uncovered floor strewn with a daily coating of sawdust, easily obtained from the local timber yards. The taproom also featured an item, now long out of memory, a cast iron spittoon.

Forester's Arms is the third building on the left, with a lamp. Next door but one was the Swan, then the Standard showing a sign board. Post 1906.

The bar and the back and front bar parlours were, as would be expected, more comfortable and better furnished. These bars provided a small step up the social scale for the minority of drinkers who used them. They were furnished with, among other items, mahogany dining tables, rush and leather chairs and framed maps of Sussex on the walls.

The front parlour had in addition an 'American Clock' and games including cribbage, bagatelle, dominoes, cards and dice.

Draught beer was served from two four-pull beer engines in the bar. Customers using the parlours were served by a waiter, whilst tap room customers had to fetch their own beer which they purchased through a serving hatch in the passage.

Accommodation for lodgers varied. The cheaper 'attick' rooms on the top floor were furnished with straw palliasses (straw mattresses) on basic beds standing on bare floors. In these 'attick' rooms lodgers were expected to follow the common practice of sharing a bed.

The first floor bedrooms, on the other hand, had feather mattresses on four poster beds standing on carpeted floors with extras, such as framed pictures, a looking glass, curtains and bell pulls. The total furniture and fittings of the Dolphin were valued at £109. 18s 6d [£109.92p] and the stock at £14. 8s 6d [£14.42p].[2]

Edwin Pulford, landlord from 1861 to 1865, had a reputation as a furniture maker and for the Romney Marsh eels he served in his kitchen. During these four years he used the back parlour as a workshop where he employed lodgers making chairs.[3]

In 1865 the next landlord renamed the Dolphin as the Forester's. A second valuation in 1870 revealed little change except that the front bar parlour now contained a Spinning Jenny board attached to the ceiling. This game consisted of a round wooden board divided into equal segments with a metal pointer. Each segment had a number or symbol. The metal pointer was spun and the highest score won. In other parts of the country it was known as Twister. In the Red Lion, Rye it was almost certainly called the Wheel of Fortune.

Spinning Jenny board

By now the Forester's had fallen in status, and had become recognised as a 'common lodging house', used by 'tramping tradesmen', hop pickers, hawkers, various itinerants and quite often several females.

Conditions of life and living at the Forester's are revealed in a report of an inquest in 1884 into the death of a travelling shoemaker, named William Chambers. After his body had been viewed by the jury the following evidence was given: Doctor J A Woodams deposed: "I was called to the Forester's Arms Inn yesterday at about 11 am and there saw the deceased lying on his back on the floor of a back room. The body was warm, but life was extinct. I examined the body but could find no marks of violence. From enquiry I made of the woman who was present at his death, I should say he died of heart disease. He came to me the previous morning and asked for a rest in the workhouse as he was not well. I replied I could not give him an order and he left. I did not see him again."

Harriet Elizabeth Craven said : "I am a widow and lodge at the Forester's Arms. I have been there about a fortnight. Deceased was lodging there when I went there. Yesterday morning about 10 o'clock I was in the kitchen when deceased came in. He sat down by the fire on a stool. About 10.45 he said, 'I wish I knew where the Relieving Officer lives'. I replied that I did not know. He said he did not think he could get out to find him. I then went to the window. I then heard him make a queer noise in his throat. I turned around and went to him. He had slipped off the stool and I drew him away from the fire. I held him with one arm and rapped on the boards for assistance. The landlord, Mr Taylor, came. Deceased was dead then. He never complained to me about anything. He was a quiet man. I never heard him quarrel with anyone."

Barnabus Taylor, landlord said: "I knew deceased as having lodged at my house for 16 or 17 days. I went into the kitchen. I looked at the deceased and said, 'he is dead'. I undid his collar and necktie. I got a man to help lay deceased on the floor on some canvas, and sent for Doctor Woodhams. The last three or four days deceased complained of his breath in going upstairs. There is nothing to lead me to suppose he died from violence."

Richard Davis, a bootmaker in Lion Street, said: "Deceased had worked for me for about three weeks. I discharged him on the previous Saturday in consequence of his not being well enough to do his work properly. I noticed the previous Monday he looked strange, as if he was having a kind of fit. I went to the Forester's Arms yesterday and saw the deceased. I paid him 12s a week while he worked for me." The jury returned a verdict of 'death from heart disease'.[4]

Eleven years later in 1895, landlord William Watts lost his licence for 'permitting drunkenness on a licensed premises', in a case that attracted much local attention. The customer in question was drunk on arrival at the Forester's and the landlord refused to serve him. However, the court took the view that although he was not served the landlord was still guilty for allowing him onto the premises.

One witness admitted there were other public houses in the locality to which he might have gone before his arrival at the Forester's, namely the Swan and the Standard next door and other pubs not far away. But witness was adamant they were in the Forester's. Another witness Councillor Deacon, was a local temperance campaigner.

Ten years later the police claimed that 'the house was unnecessary for the requirements of the neighbourhood', and in 1906 it was forced to close.[5]

The Forester's last landlord, Alfred Skinner, had only recently taken the licence. Ironically, he came to Rye from Folkestone where he had another pub which had also been forced to close. Thus within the space of a few months Arthur Skinner was twice victim of the 1904 Licensing Act. Whether or not he was doubly compensated is not recorded. After the closure of the Forester's the building reverted back to a private residence.

Forester's today

George Inn
High Street

George Inn and horse drawn omnibus. Sign board on near right says 'Bait and livery stables.' Late 19th century.

Adam's pre-war guides to Rye describe the George as the town's oldest hotel and former inn. Originally located in Market Street from 1575, it moved to its present site in the High Street in about 1720.

The building is a large structure and roughly L-shaped. Contained within the two sides of the building is a yard which in the 1770s was thought to be the site of a cockpit. A main feature on the High Street side of the building is the first floor Assembly Room, which opened in 1818 to host gatherings of farmers on market days and municipal celebrations. It subsequently became a major auction house for East Sussex.

On the ground floor, beneath the Assembly Room, is the location of the entrance to the former 'livery and bait stables' and ostlers entrance to the tap room in Lion Street. The opening of the Assembly Room boosted the status of the George from 'a dirty seaport inn' to one of Rye's most prominent licensed premises.

Between 1781 and 1794 Colonel John Byng made a series of personal journeys throughout different parts of England, and in 1788, accompanied by a companion, arrived in East Sussex. Although Byng rode a 'poney' his companion walked so they were sometimes separated until they reached their lodgings. By evening they were 'descending by a sea view all at once, into the picturesque town of Rye, by an ancient gateway; which is built upon a rock, clustered with houses, having the appearance of a fortified place'.

Bill-head 1772

"Like other maritime towns", he said, "it smells of fish and punch - by a bad pavement I came to the George, a dirty seaport inn, with a wretched stable; where in a back parlour sat I.D [was he in the Tap?], hardly glad to see me, so discontented with his treatment at this house. He said that we must go on and that a man was ready with our baggage."

Byng would have preferred to stay, feeling they might do even worse elsewhere, and reflected "never quarrel with your bread and butter". They looked around the town a little, but "as we were on such bad terms with our inn, the sooner we were gone the better, though only against my will was this refitting for an unexpected march; but our baggage had gone and I my sheets must follow".[1]

His travel companion, referred to only as 'I D', was the noted 18th century mathematician and surveyor Isaac Dalby who at the time was hard at work mapping the south-east coast for the Board of Ordnance, the defence ministry of the day.

The government realised the significance of Dalby's work and attached great importance to it. The coast had to be accurately mapped and understood in order to defend it against invasion. The survey, later the basis of the ordnance survey, meant that Dalby was a regular visitor to Sussex during the following years.

John Byng   Isaac Dalby

They continued their journey to Winchelsea with Dalby taking the footpath. Byng however, took the causeway passing Camber Castle. As he approached Winchelsea he 'surveyed with pleasure, though the evening was so bad and almost dusk, the two towns, the one, Rye upon a bare rock, the other Winchelsea upon a wooded point, both springing out of the flat; looking like two cities in Chinese paintings'. On the following days they travelled to Hastings where they stayed at the Swan before moving on to Battle and Lewes.

Yet another link between the George and the Swan, Hastings, came in the mid 19th century when perhaps the most famous function held at the George was a banquet for the Lord Mayor of London in 1850. This was not a 'state visit' but a return invitation between mayors. In 1849 Hastings resident and banker Thomas Farncombe became Lord Mayor of London. One of his first actions was to invite the Mayors of Hastings and Rye to the Mansion House.

RYE HARMONIC SOCIETY.
GEORGE HOTEL, ASSEMBLY ROOMS.
PROGRAMME for WEDNESDAY Evening, November 9th, 1859.

PART I.

VALSE.—"The Princess Royal" .... D'Albert.
SONG.—(Mr. Plant) "Mary of Argyle" ...... Nelson.
POLKA.—"The Enchantress" .... Juliano.
GLEE.—"The Red Cross Knight" .... Callcott.
QUADRILLE.—"Travatia" .... D'Albert
SONG.—(Mr. Plant) "My Pretty Jane" ...... Bishop.
OVERTURE.—"Guy Mannering" .... Bishop.
DUETT.—(Messrs. Plant and Lyon) "Is it thus
    we meet again" .... Glover.

PART II.

QUADRILLE.—"The New World" .... Marriot.
SONG.—(Mr. Plant) "Ever of Thee" .... Hall.
POLKA.—"The Rose of the Valley" .... Farmer.
GLEE.—"King Canute" .... Macfarren
VALSE.—"The Maid of the Valley" .... Farmer.
SONG.—(Mr. Plant) "Annie, dear, good bye" Wallace.
OVERTURE —"Artaxerxes" .... Dr. Arne.
FINALE —"God Save the Queen" ....
Non-Residents admitted on the payment of One Shilling.

Concert programme 1859

GEORGE HOTEL,

HIGH STREET, RYE,
SUSSEX.

FLY · **PROPRIETOR.**

JOB · **MASTER.**

LIVERY STABLE KEEPER.

W. COWTAN,

PROPRIETOR

OF the above Old-Established Commercial and Family Hotel, having recently added to his Posting Business

A NEW CANOE-SHAPED FUNERAL CAR,

of the latest design and suited to the requirements of the present day, which can be used open or closed—built by J. BLIGH AND SON, of Ramsgate—hopes, by punctuality and moderate charges, to merit a share of that business.

W.C. takes this opportunity of thanking his numerous customers for their patronage.

W.C. also begs to submit a List of Prices of Spirits of good age, and well-matured :—

Gin - -	2s 0d,	2s 6d,	2s 8d	3s 0d per Bottle.
Pale Brandy - -	3s 3d,	4s 0d,	5s 0d	,,
Irish or Scotch Whisky	2s 9d,	3s 3d,	3s 6d	,,
Rum - - -	2s 6d,	3s 0d,	3s 6d	,,

Larger or smaller quantities supplied.

Martell's or Hennessey's Brandies.
All Malt Liquors of the best qualities only.

BASS'S AND ROMFORD BOTTLED ALES. *GUINNESS'S BOTTLED STOUT.*

ALL ORDERS FOR ROOMS, CARRIAGES, OR ANY OF THE ABOVE GOODS CAREFULLY ATTENDED TO,

LIQUID SUNSHINE (THE FINEST RUM) 42s. per Dozen
STRATHISLA WHISKY (PUREST HIGHLAND MALT WHISKY.) 42s. ,,

TO BE OBTAINED OF:

WILLIAM COWTAN, The GEORGE HOTEL, RYE.

Advertisement 1891

In response, in April 1850, the Hastings Corporation hosted a return banquet at the Swan, Hastings to honour their most famous resident. This was followed by a second banquet in May, organised by the Rye Corporation, at the George.[2]

Two years later during the General Election of 1852, the George is mentioned in reference to the 'treating scandal' of that year. At a House of Commons inquiry the principle witness, Mayor Jeremiah Smith, was accused of perjury. The perjured evidence concerned a dinner at the George given for the retiring Member of Parliament and his successor.

Smith told the Election Committee of the House of Commons on oath, that the dinner had been paid for by the MP to avoid associating the new candidate's name with 'treating'. But it came out that the dinner was paid for by the new candidate through an intermediary who went 'to a certain couch in the back bar of the Red Lion where, under a certain cushion' he found £230 to pay for the dinner at the George. Smith was subsequently imprisoned for a year.[3]

c1895

A good example of advertising the medicinal qualities of alcohol 1909. The label on the bottle says 'Each pint contains the energizing carbohydrates of 10 ozs of pure dairy milk. Invigorating and stimulating. An ideal beverage for the rheumatic invalid and all workers. Mackeson and Co. Ltd, Hythe Brewery, Kent.'

1950

George Tap
Lion Street

George Tap on right c1900

The George Tap was originally the public bar of the inn, with the additional functions of servicing the coach drivers, ostlers and stablemen who worked there, plus any servants who arrived with hotel guests.

The George was at one time a centre of cockfighting, although probably not the only one. To give one of several examples: In 1769 the Kentish Gazette advertised a cockfight organised by one Abraham Smith: 'at the George Inn, Rye; the Bull's Head, Battle and the Swan Inn, Hastings'. This was a tournament circulating between these three inns, with 11 cocks in each of two teams.

Cockfighting had a very strong appeal among the gambling fraternity, and the prize money contributed by the owners of the fighting cocks, was very high. The stakes for this cockfight were four guineas (£270 today) for each of 10 fights and 10 guineas (£680 today) 'for the final battle'. We can only imagine the frenzy of activity at the George as customers placed their bets in the parlour or in the taproom before rushing off to view the disturbing spectacle.

As was common in those days each of these three venues would have had their own cockpit nearly always located outside. In the case of the George the cockpit was almost definitely located in the tap courtyard, although we cannot rule out a cockpit inside the building. Cockfighting remained legal until 1835 when it was banned. Thus in all probability it continued in Rye after 1769.[1]

By 1800 there were several carriers operating from the George Tap to London, and to towns and villages all over East Sussex. 'Walker's Light Cart starts from the George every Wednesday and delivers parcels to Ashford, Appledore, Barham, Battle Beckley, Brookland, Canterbury, Dymchurch, Folkstone, Ham Street, Hastings, Hawkhurst, Iden, Peasmarsh, Romney, Robertsbridge, Sandgate and Winchelsea.'

The *1798 Street Directory* listed: 'John Marchant of Hawkhurst, common carrier, arrives at the George Inn on Saturdays about ten in the morning and returns to Hawkhurst the same evening; sets out from thence on Tuesday mornings and arrives at the White Hart, Borough Wednesday noon, and sets out from thence early on Thursday morning, and arrives at Hawkhurst on Friday.'

Over the years several incidents have been recorded in the Tap. In 1767 a report on the 'The Unruly Behaviour of John Shurley' tells us that a customer called John Shurley came into the kitchen attached to the George Tap, and in a heated exchange started waving his stick about which broke a pot hanging from a shelf. When told by the landlord, Edward Sayers, that he would have to pay for it, a quarrel broke out over how much. Another customer, 'a dealer in those wares', said the price was 13d. John Shurley then called Mrs Shurley, who was in the garden, for her opinion. 'Sixpence', she said at which point John Shurley became aggressive towards the landlord. 'The landlord had to hold him by the collar and would not let go.'[2]

Again in 1806 we are informed of another incident, this time involving a female customer, a soldier and a police constable. The police constable, Edward Basson was examined by the mayor, George Lamb and a Justice of the Peace. Basson described on oath how he went into the George Tap to apprehend a woman charged with felony whom, he had been informed, was drinking in the bar. He was about to take her into custody when: 'William Uncles a private in Captain James Troop of the Royal Waggon Train interposed, and prevented him by violence furthering his act into execution.' The constable went back to the George Tap a second time, and was about to apprehend the woman 'when the said William Uncles threatened to knock him down'. When Uncles was arrested for threatening behaviour and obstruction, he assaulted the constable 'and gave him several blows'.[3]

And in 1872 yet another:

CHARGE AGAINST A SOLDIER

Robert Dodds, a private in the King's Own Regiment, was charged with stealing three £1 notes, the property of an employee at the George Hotel, Rye.

Prosecutrix said accused had been a frequent customer since the soldiers arrived at the town, with some other friends, during the past fortnight. She only knew him as an ordinary customer. She missed three £1 notes last Saturday afternoon. She had kept them in a purse in a bag underneath the counter in the small bar in the taproom. This was at the George Hotel tap. She had never seen prisoner on her side of the counter. She might have used the bag in his presence, because she never had any mistrust of anybody. She informed the Manager of the loss, and was advised to go to the Superintendent of Police. The Superintendent showed her two £1 notes. Prosecutrix did not remember the numbers of her notes. She saw accused on Saturday afternoon after she had missed the notes. Accused denied taking any notes.

P.C. Boniface, of Playden, said that at 3.30 p.m. on the previous Saturday he received information that the notes had been stolen from the George Hotel tap. With Superintendent Whitlock he made enquiries and saw the prisoner. P.S. Whitlock asked prisoner if he had been in the George Hotel tap that day. Accused replied that he had not been there till that afternoon, but afterwards he admitted that he had been there at two pm. P.S. Whitlock told accused they were making enquiries about some money missing from the George Hotel tap. Accused said he had not taken any money from the George tap, and he was willing to be searched. With that he went into some stables close by and emptied his pockets. He emptied 5s. 6½d. out of a trouser pocket, and letters, etc., out of a tunic pocket. He said, "That is all the money I had on me". P.S. Whitlock told him it was paper money they were making enquiries about, not loose cash. He replied, "Oh, I have not got any paper money on me". They searched the letters etc., and found one £1 note rolled up amongst the letters. They took accused to the Police Station, and he was again searched, and another £1 note was found rolled up in the bottom of his trousers. The hem of the trousers had been split, and the note put in. Accused was then charged with stealing the notes; he made a rambling reply. Accused asked no questions of witness.[4]

For most of the 19th century the George Tap was a simple beer house licensed separately from the hotel. This was common practice in the 19th century when beer house keepers were usually the under tenant of the fully licensed hotel landlord.

This arrangement allowed the hotel landlord to farm out the responsibility for the tap room but still reap the benefits of the 1830 beer act [see introduction]. The George Tap was run separately from the hotel from at least 1824 and probably a lot earlier until sometime in the 1870s. It is now a fully integrated part of the hotel.

George Public Bar 1950

Entrance to the George yard today

Globe
Military Road

The Globe opened in 1834 when a 50 year lease on this piece of land was granted to John Wheeler by the Reverend Lamb of Iden. John Wheeler, a beer retailer, then became the Globe's first landlord. The lease included the cliff behind the pub which descends from Playden Heights, with its 'pendants [overhanging parts] being part and parcel of the property'. A fairly large cave in the face of the cliff at the rear of the building was also included in the lease. The annual rent was £127.[1]

Four years later, in 1838, the pub was put on the market and sold after John Wheeler had emigrated to Canada. At that time the Globe consisted of two parlours, a bar, tap room, skittle alley at the rear and four bedrooms to let.

THE GLOBE INN, RYE, SUSSEX

TO BE SOLD BY PRIVATE CONTRACT, the above Inn, which was built in 1834, and contains two front parlours, tap-room, bar, kitchen, with a large oven, and five excellent bedchambers, besides an excellent skittle ground, and garden, well stocked with fruit trees, containing upwards of a quarter of an acre. The whole of the premises are situate immediately between and adjoining the London and Dover roads, and in a new and improving part of the town of Rye. The above Inn is in full trade, and immediate possession may be had, as the proprietor is about to emigrate.

The premises are held under a lease, at a small annual ground rent, and 46 years will be unexpired at Michaelmas next.

The purchaser will have power to sell or remove all erections and buildings at the expiration of the term.

For further particulars apply to Mr CARPENTER, Solicitor, Rye; or to the Proprietor, on the premises (all letters to be post-paid).

1838 [2]

In its early days the Globe was used by men employed on the maintenance of the Royal Military Canal which flows nearby, and after which Military Road is named. A sketch map of the canal from the 1830s shows the Globe as an isolated building in a totally rural setting.

By the 1860s adjacent outbuildings had become a forge and blacksmith's shop later known as Sutton's Forge, which is now the car park. Stables were established at the back as was an ever popular and now larger skittle alley. By now the Globe was using the old cave in the cliff face as the pub cellar. The Globe cave cellar became a feature in Rye's official guide books published by Adams throughout the 1930s.

The popularity of Friendly Societies in 19th century Rye led the Globe to set up the Globe Friendly Society in 1872 which immediately joined in with other societies in the town in the annual Rye Gala Day

Sutton's forge and the Globe Inn

celebrations. The Globe Friendly Society had its own club room in one of the original parlours and over the next 15 years grew steadily in size. The society seems to have existed for about 15 years until about 1887 when it went into abeyance.[3]

The Globe's most popular and longstanding landlord was Marshall Ames, a busy and energetic man who ran the Globe for 40 years from 1859–1899. As well as the Globe, he also had a building company involved in the development of the area in the last 30 years of the 19th century. In 1887 Ames's building employees were entertained to a sumptuous dinner in the Globe by a Mr Hills of Playden on the completion of his new house.

When Marshall Ames died in 1899 the licence was transferred to Emily Ames, who ran the pub until 1903. Thus, the Ames family ran the Globe from 1859 to 1903, a period of 44 years. The Globe is therefore, the longest held family run pub in Rye.

The winding up of the Globe Friendly Society in the late 1880s was followed, in 1899, by the arrival of a new branch of the Tunbridge Wells and South-East Equitable Society, then setting up local branches in East Sussex. This branch operated out of the Globe for nine years until 1908 when, 'because of an increased membership and the need for more space', it moved to the Crown in Ferry Road.[4]

Another club which came into existence at the turn of the century was the Globe Horticultural Club. Not surprisingly, in an area of cottage gardens and developing allotments, the subject of gardening among Globe customers was always a popular topic of conversation in the bar. Garden produce was first brought into the pub in about 1898, and from then on displays, particularly of flowers, were a regular Globe feature.

"The origin of the flower show was a squabble", said the club chairman in 1903, "perhaps I ought to call it a discussion, as to who could grow the best dahlias. The discussion was a hot one and in the end we decided to have a Dahlia Show to see who could produce the best. After this we formed a Dahlia Club, later a Dahlia and Daffodil Club and from that it became the Globe Horticultural Club. I think that there is no town the size of Rye that could get a show better than ours in the winter months...."[5] However, the club had serious competition from the Rye Gardeners who met and displayed garden produce at the Cinque Ports Arms.

In 1905 the local press commented:-

The healthy, profitable, and fascinating pursuit of cottage gardening was the all-absorbing theme at the Globe Inn on Tuesday evening, when the members and friends of the Globe Horticultural Club assembled on the occasion of their annual dinner. The old town of Rye is well served with organisations whose aim is to encourage gardening amongst cottagers in the district, and there are many who think that an amalgamation would be beneficial to all concerned. However this may be, the Globe Horticultural Club has done its part in promoting keen and friendly rivalry amongst the working classes. During the summer and autumn months many excellent exhibits are staged at the Globe shows, and last year many specimens of fruit and vegetables shown were really remarkable, thus showing that the cottagers must have devoted a considerable amount of study to the various plants in order to discover the secrets of nature. This Club has sufficiently demonstrated its usefulness to commend it to the patronage of those interested in horticulture and the welfare of the working classes. We hope the Society, which has an enthusiastic president in Mr. Harry Davis, will meet with continued success.[6]

In 1898, the Globe became the headquarters of a branch of the Bonfire Boys, who by 1905 were known as the Military Road Bonfire Boys, to distinguish themselves from other groups in the town. This group and one or two others established in Rye around 1900, were the antithesis, the direct opposite, of the Bonfire Boys which had plagued Rye for much of the 19th century. One writer described this as "the taming of the Bonfire Boys".[7]

Throughout these years the Military Road Bonfire Boys were involved in charity events for Hastings hospital as well as organising for the 'fifth', until the onset of the First World War when the group went into suspension.

After the war the Globe gradually re-established itself. It was now tied to the Style and Winch Brewery of Maidstone and became one of the first Rye pubs to have a darts team. By 1925 it was a vigorous member of the Rye Darts League competing for the Style and Winch Challenge Cup.

The Globe today

Another new club, the Rye Angling Club, was set up at the Globe in 1925. Its members fished in the Royal Military Canal and in the gravel pits around Rye harbour. With a break during the Second World War this club continued into the 1960s, but later transferred to the Bedford Arms.

The Globe Inn 1870 with the Forge on the site of present Car Park

THE GLOBE INN
MILITARY ROAD RYE

Globe Inn, Military Road, Rye, a Courage & Barclay House. All beer drawn from the wood. Car Park and garden for children. Wedding Receptions catered for. Accommodation Bed & Breakfast. Personal service of Mr. & Mrs. R. E. Bignell

Telephone  Rye 2180

The cave cellar, a natural cave in what were once the Cliffs of England

1960

Greyhound
Wish Street

1890

The earliest known date for the Greyhound as a licensed premises is 1838. Prior to that date there was an un-named beer house in Wish Street which might have been a predecessor of the Greyhound.

One of the Greyhound's longest serving landlords was John Myers who took over in 1852, the year of a General Election and the 'treating scandal'. Incredibly for such a small pub, the Greyhound was given a total of £25 (in today's terms £1,400) worth of free beer!

It seems that John Myers had a bad name with the local authorities and was not trusted by the police. In 1859 he was fined for allowing a savage bull dog to roam free in the Greyhound yard, and in 1861 he complained that the police searched the Greyhound, including the bedrooms 'looking for a stolen sheep'!

Getting a living from running this pub had, by the 1860s, become a precarious business, and in 1863 the Greyhound closed down after John Myers became bankrupt.

John Myers of Rye in the County of Sussex, a Licensed Victualler and Dealer in Fishing Nets and Marine Stores ... was adjudged bankrupt ... on the 14th May 1863 and is required to surrender to William Hazlett, Registrar ... at the said meeting of creditors, and a second meeting in June for a last examination.[1]

After eight months the brewery finally managed to find another tenant and reopened the Greyhound in early 1864. It was then a favourite haunt of the military, particularly members of the Royal Artillery, who were stationed near Martello Tower number 28 at Rye harbour.

Their custom however, often led to conflict. One evening in 1873 Gunner James Gaunt called into the Greyhound Tap for a glass of ale. Shortly afterwards William Rhodes came in and accused him of boasting that Rhodes wife had 'scored him up 10s worth of beer in the Pipemakers', which led to an assault.

Whether Rhodes thought his wife had been buying beer for the soldier or whether he thought they had had an association behind his back is unclear. But the case does reveal a further example of pub 'scoring' ie the system of credit used in pubs and in this case by a woman.[2]

In 1891 a drunken customer fell asleep in the skittle alley:

ONE MAN AND HIS DOG
William Burgess was charged with being drunk and incapable on
the premises of the Greyhound Inn, Rye, on March 21st. – P.C.
W H Breech stated that from information received he went to the
Greyhound Inn on the day named, and found Burgess in the skittle
alley in a helpless condition, and the landlady requested him to
remove him. This he was unable to do until he had secured the
defendant's dog, which would not permit him to approach its
owner. Having done this he obtained a handcart, and by that
means conveyed Burgess to the lock-up, where he was detained by
Sergt. Read till the following morning. – Defendant, who handed
in a letter from his mother, pleading for lenient treatment, stated
that a little beer soon overcame him, and promised that he would
keep away from the drink in future. – The Mayor said that they
would deal leniently with him, not for his own sake, but for his
mother's. He had heard him give the same promise before. A
previous conviction was proved against him on March 31st, 1890,
and he, therefore, by one day, escaped the heavier penalty. – Fined
*2s. 6d. and costs, or in default seven days imprisonment.*3

In 1892 Herbert Verral Chapman, brewer of East Guildford, agreed a lease with the owner of the property, Ursula Hawkes of Chatham, for 'all that messuage, tenement or inn called the Greyhound situate in Wish Street, Rye ... and now in the occupation of Rebecca Hubbard together, with stables, outhouses, buildings and rights of way ... for 25 years at a rent of £18 per year'. A covenant in the lease stipulated that the building could only be used for the purpose of an inn or public house and could not be used as a private house, or for any other purpose.[4]

One of the last landlords was Thomas Mannering who, in 1905, had to summons a customer for refusing to 'quit the pub', and for an assault on the landlady. The customer went into the taproom, where there were seven or eight men drinking, called for a pint of beer and, in a loud voice, started an argument with some soldiers. The landlady tapped him on the shoulder and asked him to be quiet. The man then struck her in the chest and the police were called.

In court a lawyer facetiously advising him said: "The Greyhound landlady is a good sized woman and well able to defend herself and you are a poor, miserable little man", [laughter in court]. "You ought to have taken out a cross summons for assault." However, after this sexist 'witticism' from his lawyer he was fined 5s [25p].[5]

After this case Thomas Mannering gave up the Greyhound or, more probably was dismissed by the brewery, and within the next six months two more landlords tried but failed to keep the pub in business. One of them was conductor of the Rye Town Band.

In 1906 the Greyhound, which had been trading as a public house for 68 years and probably longer as a beer house, became one of the first victims in Rye of the new powers available to local magistrates under the 1904 Licensing Act, and was closed down.

The grounds of police opposition were:-
1. That a fully licensed house in the place where the premises are situate is not required.
2. Having regard to the character and interests of the neighbourhood, the number of licensed houses in the vicinity, the licence held in respect of such premises is unnecessary.
3. That in the interests of the public the renewal of the licence is undesirable.[6]

Over the next five years the Greyhound was joined by three other 'undesirable' pubs: the Foresters Arms, the Swan and the Borough Arms and also the town's last two remaining beer houses, the Oak and the London Stout House.

Both the owners, Chapman's brewery and the licensee, were financially compensated. A short time after this the Greyhound was converted into a private residence and sold.

In the following year, 1907, the freehold, the cottage and the other property at the rear of the premises, 'recently known as the Greyhound', was also sold by Ursula Hawkes to Henry Gasson of Rye.

The Greyhound was located on the side of a small lane, probably a right of way. Sometime after its closure it was converted into two cottages. The cottages, long since gone, were later replaced by a pair of semi-detached houses.

The name Greyhound is a common pub name which has been traced to the old English 'Gre-hundr grech' or 'greg', meaning dog, and 'hundr', meaning hunting. Another possibility is that greyhounds came from Greece, and came to be called 'Greek hounds'. So the name may in fact be a derivation of Greek hound.

Adams Guide to Rye for 1934 provides a local explanation and attributes the name to a Rye legend which states that the pub took its name from the Greyhound Yard at the rear of the building which has 'had this name since 1588 when no person was permitted to keep a dog except a greyhound'. However, there is no corroboration of this dubious tale. Alternatively, the name might have derived from a schooner of the same name built in Rye in the mid 19th century.

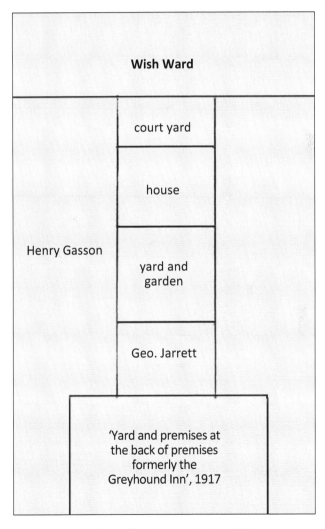

Greyhound yard ground plan 1917

CHAPMAN BROTHERS,

BREWERS,

WHOLESALE WINE & SPIRIT MERCHANTS,

R Y E .

PROPRIETORS OF

RYE MILK PUNCH

AND

ROMNEY MARSH SLOE GIN,

SPECIAL DRINKS FOR THE WINTER SEASON.

Blenders of old Scotch and Irish Whiskies.

'Winter drinks' sold at the Greyhound in the late 19th century

Site of the Greyhound today

Hope & Anchor
Watchbell St

Late 19th century

The Hope & Anchor is housed in a medieval building dating from the 15th century. At least part of the premises are built over a barrel vaulted cellar connected to the Gascony wine trade. However, its modern use as a licensed premises dates from the 1830s.

In 1838 the premises were listed in the commercial section of the Street Directory as a Beer Retailer (ie beer house). It was not included in the town's 'Inns and Public Houses' section until an entry in *Piggott's Directory* for 1839. This indicates that the house was now fully licensed and had acquired the name Hope & Anchor.

As a public house frequented by the fishing community and popular with mariners and boatmen, its tap room (the former beer house) remained separately licensed until at least the 1870s, enabling the proprietor to take advantage of the 1830 Beer Act. The beer house keeper of the Hope & Anchor was most likely the under tenant of the fully licensed landlord. The George Hotel and Tap had a similar arrangement.

The Amicable Mariners Benefit Society was founded and established here in 1843, but moved to the Crown, Ferry Road when landlord Isaac Wright changed pubs and moved to the Crown in 1859. The society then had 20 members but by 1861 the membership had doubled to 40. Their Secretary was F Crowhurst and their Medical Officer Dr J Adamson.

From 1849 to 1856 the Hope & Anchor hosted groups of men employed by Rye Corporation on local public work, and paid for by vouchers issued by the Chamberlain. Other customers were employed in the shipyards working on vessels for the Crimean War from 1853 to 1856, and of course there were many fishermen who drank here.

In 1905 a commentator looking back over 50 years said: "In those days the fishermen, and others connected with the town whose employment was largely dependent on favourable winds and weather, had certain rendezvous such as 'the Green', Watchbell Street, in front of the Hope & Anchor public house then kept by a well known character, 'Ikey' (Isaac) Wright to wit; the corner near the blacksmith's forge at Landgate and the East Cliff near the business establishment then conducted by a cordwainer known as Jimmy May."

RYE ... RYE

SHIPWRIGHTS V. SHIPWRIGHTS.

A GRAND MATCH OF

Cricket

WILL BE PLAYED ON THE

TOWN SALTS, RYE,

on MONDAY, JULY 16th, 1849,

BETWEEN ELEVEN SHIPWRIGHTS OF

Messrs. Hoad Brothers,

AND ELEVEN SHIPWRIGHTS OF

MESSRS. HESSELL AND HOLMES,

FOR TEN SOVEREIGNS.

WICKETS TO BE PITCHED AT ONE O'CLOCK.

A GOOD SUPPER will be provided, at the HOPE & ANCHOR INN, for the players, in the evening, and for any friend who may be pleased to honour them with their company,

by the puplic's obedient servant.

EDWARD FOWLE.

H. P. Clark, Printer, Rye

In 1852 the Hope & Anchor was one of the pubs which provided free food and drink during the 'treating scandal' of the General Election of that year. In the Hope & Anchor club room and bars, customers managed to consume £22. 3s worth of free food and drink. [£1,299 in today's terms!]

When Isaac Wright transferred to the Crown in 1859, the Hope & Anchor premises and contents were subject to a valuation for the incoming tenant. The public rooms then consisted of a club room, great parlour, bar parlour, a bar and a taproom. Bedrooms or chambers are mentioned in the valuation but it seems they were unused, which tells us that the premises were in use as a public house but did not provide accommodation at that time.[1]

After 1860 the house suffered from a run of bad luck, and over the next four years, six different individuals held the licence. These included two representatives from Chapman's East Guildford brewery filling in, when they were unable find a licensee.

In 1862 there was an incident between sawyers who had been drinking all night at a 'Free and Easy', where fishermen met to relax, smoke, drink and sing. 'Free and Easies' were run by a chairman and were open to anyone who could afford a pipe, a pint of beer and who was willing to sing.

The Tap Room was still licensed separately from the main premises, with its own beer house keeper Edwin Swaddling. In 1862 there were at least two incidents involving Swaddling and his customers, one of whom was a member of the coastguard.[2]

The following year in 1863, 22-year old Mary Jane Collins was refused a licence for the main premises as the magistrates thought she was too young to cope. Subsequently in 1864 the pub 'closed for a considerable time' before being re-licensed under a new landlord.

But bad luck continued to dog the Hope & Anchor throughout the 1870s. Stephen Smith, another beer house keeper who formerly ran another beer house in the High Street, took over the tap in about 1878 but was prosecuted by the police for serving 'persons of notorious bad character' ie prostitutes.[3]

By 1878 the premises were in use as a lodging house by labourers working on the sea wall, and in 1879 landlord Edward Skinner was charged with having his house open at 12.30am on a Sunday morning. A constable claimed that whilst searching the premises he found one of the Rye harbour pilots hiding in a bed, fully clothed, and chased a second customer across the pub rooftop. The customer escaped by shinning down a drainpipe and ran off into the night, leaving the constable stranded on the roof out of breath! The harbour pilot later admitted he was in the house after hours but claimed he was only drinking 'a ginger warmer after working a tide'![4]

On a more serious note there was a suicide attempt in the bar in 1881 when the landlord's son attempted to cut his throat. In the shocking scene which followed there was a lot of blood, but his life was saved by quick witted customers who removed their coats and scarves to tourniquet his neck. Luckily, a passing doctor also gave assistance.[5]

After this, Mackeson's Hythe Brewery gave up on the Hope & Anchor, and in the same year, 1881, the premises were put up for auction at the George. As a 'free and fully licensed' business it was purchased for £330 by Brighton brewer James Body.[6] Apart from brewing, James Body was also a well known international wrestling champion with a 'no nonsense' reputation.

The James Body Brewery was bought out by the Hodges and Ritchie Brewery of Rye in 1882, and then by the Bowen Brewery of Rye in 1890.

These changes of ownership seem to have provided a new direction and turning point. Tied to a new brewery and with a new landlord, the Hope & Anchor's fortunes began to revive, and from then until the First World War its status improved. This may have been due to the fact that for the next 17 years all the licensees were female.

From the end of the First World War into the 1920s the Hope & Anchor was not listed in the street directory and seems to have been closed. In 1925 it was re-opened as a 'greatly enlarged new hotel' with electricity and central heating in all 10 bedrooms, which were personalised with name plates painted by a local artist. A vegetarian menu was introduced which was possibly the first in Rye.[7]

The name was changed to 'Hope Anchor' as the conjunction 'and' was thought to be incorrect. In Christian symbolism an 'anchor' is a symbol of hope. To mariners and those who go to sea the spare anchor is known as the 'Hope Anchor'.

At least one source suggested that: 'A fine modern hotel has been erected on the site of the old Hope & Anchor Inn', and another remarked: 'There is little left of its former characteristics, brick floors and general discomforts'.

Under the proprietorship of Miss C Bellhouse, the premises became the home of a local literary group known as the Anchorites, who met here for lectures and discussion, and also the venue for craft fairs. During the inter-war years the Hope Anchor was the inspiration for the 'Traders Arms, Curfew Street', in the Mapp and Lucia novels by E F Benson.

In the Second World War the hotel was requisitioned by the Royal Sussex Regiment and suffered some blast damage from German bombs, but was not destroyed. Today its striking façade dominates the western side of the town.

Hope Anchor today

Jolly Sailor
Watchbell Street

c1900

The Jolly Sailor first opened its doors as a beer house in Watchbell Street in 1830. Landlord Thomas Hearsfield applied immediately for a full licence in 1831, and again successfully in 1832. Both applications were supported by a petition organised by local vicar John Myer who was Rye mayor in 1828. He urged the magistrates to consider:

> *That your petitioner has legally settled in the said town, has a wife and three small children wholly dependant on him for support. That your petitioner has opened his house under the late act for the sale of beer, which has been regularly conducted by him without any complaint from his neighbours or any other persons whomsoever. Your petitioner begs leave to state that there is no licensed public house in Watchbell Street and the nearest one is the Red Lion. That your petitioner has been informed and believes it to be true that the public in general would be better accommodated if the house of your petitioner were licensed as a regular public house and that he has been advised to apply for the same and has in pursuance of such advice caused the regular notices to be given of his intentions of making such application. He therefore most humbly prays your worships will be pleased to take his case into your consideration and grant the necessary certificate that will enable him to apply to the excise for the necessary license and should your petitioner succeed he hereby most faithfully promises to keep as regular a house in all respects as he has before done. And your petitioner states John Hearsfield is a fit person to keep a public house.*[1]

Notwithstanding the support of the vicar and 45 residents, within 10 years the Jolly Sailor had become a common lodging house for poor travellers and itinerants, as in 19th century Rye there was a big demand from the travelling poor for the basic accommodation the Jolly Sailor had to offer.

In 1839 John Hearsfield died leaving the Jolly Sailor and his estate to his wife Mary, who ran the pub until 1841. She also inherited two cottages located behind the pub in Hucksteps Row, and a house in Watchbell Street.

On census night 1841 the Jolly Sailor had 11 lodgers. As well as Mary Hearsfield and her two children, (perhaps the third child had died), the lodgers consisted of a shoemaker's family of four, two cap makers, a weaver, a painter, an agricultural labourer and two 'independent' women, aged 25 and 26-years old.

In the same year Mary Hearsfield left this rumbustious and high spirited pub to run a nearby shop, which remained in the Hearsfield family for the next 30 years.

"The Jolly Sailor", said Peter Ewart, "was no ordinary tavern, even in those days. Patronised by the roughest elements of the public its interior was the scene of many sinister doings during its comparatively short history."[2]

In 1841 James Dawson took over from Mary Hearsfield to become the pub's longest serving landlord, until 1874. Dawson became a well known local character and during the 1850s and '60s was often to be seen standing in the pub doorway beckoning a welcome to many a passing stranger.

Dawson was also landlord during the 'treating scandal' of 1852, when surprisingly, given the size of the house, he hosted not one, but three free dinners with free alcohol to the tune of £15. 5s 6d. In today's terms this was about £880!

The next landlord was William Watts who, like his predecessor John Hearsfield, also owned property in Hucksteps Row. A guide book points out that 'for many years these small dwellings were considered so far gone they were thought unsuitable for occupation'. But William Watts 'took an interest in them and several were in consequence restored and tenanted'.

Unfortunately for him, some of his tenants were not always on their best behaviour or the most prompt with their rent. In 1879 a group of them attempted to have him indicted for serving porter out of hours on a Sunday morning, apparently because he was demanding they pay their rent arrears.

William Watts won the case and a tenant was evicted. The case report informs us that the Jolly Sailor, even when it was 'closed' as a public house, traded fish, eels, pork and vegetables, direct from its back gate to the inhabitants of Hucksteps Row and beyond. Watts also sold porter and beer from the back door, which was carried away by the locals in earthenware jugs and bottles.[3]

Complaints about Jolly Sailor customers were regular and continuous, and the police described them at various times as

dancing bear

'gypsies, hop pickers, rag and bone collectors and those who go mushrooming on the marsh'.

The Jolly Sailor also provided accommodation for the many street entertainers who visited the town in large numbers during the second half of the 19th century. This group of customers included the owners of dancing bears, one man bands and various street musicians. While their owners slept the bears were chained and locked in a shed at the rear.

On one occasion the landlord was accused of overcrowding, and to have accommodated 30 lodgers in one night. This turned out to be false, but it was the type of rumour which fed into local folk-lore about the Jolly Sailor over the years.

Another widely circulated story was that the pub used a system of taught ropes slung across a room at chest height, for lodgers to drape themselves over in order to sleep. They were woken up in the morning by the landlady slackening the ropes!

In 1886 Thomas Marsh took over the Jolly Sailor as his first pub. He was told "the Jolly Sailor is a difficult house. Some very peculiar characters resort there at times, and great care is needed on the part of the landlord."[4]

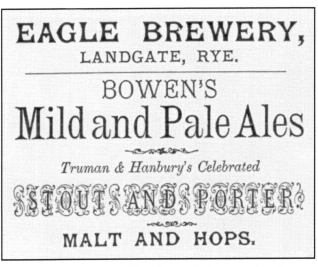

EAGLE BREWERY,

LANDGATE, RYE.

BOWEN'S
Mild and Pale Ales

Truman & Hanbury's Celebrated

STOUT AND PORTER

MALT AND HOPS.

The Jolly Sailor was tied to the Eagle Brewery, Landgate

Many an incoming landlord was advised by the magistrates of the difficulties he might encounter in the pub particularly if he was new to the town (see the Ship). In 1900 new landlord Henry Wilson was told: "This is not a first class house and it is a difficult thing for a landlord to keep his customers in order." And in 1909 the final landlord, John Best, was advised: "This house requires a great deal of supervision. You must be careful in the manner in which it is conducted." However, in 1910 the Jolly Sailor became yet another victim of the 1904 Act and was closed down.[5]

Twenty years later *Adams Guide to Rye and District* informed its readers about 'another abandoned inn – perhaps the most sinister to a bygone generation – the Jolly Sailor, which, could its walls speak, would unfold tales as sordid and crime stained as many associated with the doss houses of the Bowery. Many a person I remember being hailed from the brick floored, smoky taproom, or sparsely furnished and cheerless upper chambers, where the tramping fraternity certainly encountered some strange bed fellows.'

"In my mind's eye", said the writer, "I still see the typical landlord, James Dawson, seldom without his churchwarden,* standing at the threshold of his pub bidding welcome to all and sundry of his customers. The spartan accommodation provided was

* A clay pipe with a twenty four inch long stem.

regarded as much superior to the alternative of passing the night in the vagrant's ward of the workhouse."

The original building, now a private house, still stands and portrays feint signage from its pub days of over a century ago.

Jolly Sailor today

Kings Arms
Wish Street

1905

The Kings Arms, first known as William the Fourth, was opened as a beer house by Thomas Aylward of the Albion Brewery, sometime in the late 1820s or early 1830s.[1] Aylward seems to have been the first landlord, followed by Samuel Austin, and then George Whiteman, formerly a shop keeper of Rope Walk.

When Whiteman returned as landlord in the 1860s, he claimed he had previously held the licence as a beer house keeper (1838–1844) and also that he had been the first fully licensed landlord sometime during that period.

Several times in the 1850s there were complaints about the 'long room' in the Kings Arms, a large bar used for music and dancing. From the 1850s until the 1870s the 'long room' was a rendezvous for visiting sailors and for the military based in Rye Harbour. On several occasions there were concerns about sailors and their girl friends 'fiddling and dancing' into the early hours. "It is a very curious house", said one police constable. "If I go in one way people go through the large room and out the other!"

Another early attraction was the oyster shop located nearby. On certain evenings, particularly weekends, drinkers flocked to the William the Fourth for beer and oysters, which for a number of years was a recognised pub speciality.

An infamous character who was landlord from 1852 until 1860 was James Hobbs Star, who moved here from the short lived Albion Commercial Inn in Rope Walk. In 1859 he was charged with serving beer at 1.45am on a Sunday morning, followed by another two cases of allowing 'Persons of a Notoriously Bad Character' into the pub. In 1860 he was charged again, this time by the Inland Revenue, with 'having sold unaccounted half a gallon of gin and a pint of rum'.

He was fined £12. 10s [£12.50] for each case, after a well known police informer, William Edwards of Icklesham, gave evidence. 'A few spectators saluted Edwards with hearty groans and unmistakable expressions of opinion as he left the court. Edwards was then conducted to Rye railway station by a constable, to protect him from any harm.'[2]

After this, Hobbs Star was refused another licence and was then arrested and imprisoned for tax evasion. A letter from the Inland Revenue to the Rye authorities in 1860 requested an 'allowance of 6d per day for the support of James Hobbs Star, a revenue prisoner'. The letter was annotated: '61 days at 6 pence a day'.[3]

One of the above 'Persons of Notoriously Bad Character':—

Ann Wood, aged 25, a prostitute, was charged by police-constable Butcher with being drunk and disorderly on the previous evening. From his evidence it appeared that he found the prisoner near the 'William the Fourth', very drunk, so much so that she was obliged to be placed on a truck to convey her to the station; even this plan did not answer, and she was carried by two or three men to the gaol, alarming the whole neighbourhood as she went along.

The Mayor insisted upon knowing where she got the drink, and at length elicited that it was at the 'William the Fourth', but this was denied by a person, whose name did not transpire, who said that she was so drunk that she could not stand upright before she went there.

It seems that she came here as a hopper and during that time she lodged at the 'Ship' and conducted herself well: since then she had been leading a dissipated life, and as she had been turned out of the 'Ship' obtained a lodging for one night at the 'Queen Adelaide', and on being turned away from there she had associated with a well known character named Marchant.

The Mayor seriously admonished her on her course of life, but apparently without much effect. Sentenced to twenty-one days hard labour.[4]

In 1870 the premises was threatened by fire, and for insurance purposes an attempt was made to establish the cause. At this time the pub was patronised by 'hoppers' particularly in October. It was the custom for female hoppers to smoke clay pipes when they were taking their beer, and the police claimed that this was the cause of the fire. However, they were not able to prove the point and the pipe smoking continued.

Other 'bad characters' noted by the police apart from the hoppers, were 'ladies of the night', and 'lodgers who arrived at the pub carrying their belongings in bundles tied to sticks'. Over the next decade there seems to have been little change, and in 1879 Henry Jarrett was also charged.

Henry, John Jarrett, landlord of the William the Fourth, was charged by Supt. Bourne with permitting his house to be the resort of prostitutes, and 'allowing them to remain longer than was necessary for the obtaining of refreshments'.

Supt. Bourne said about half-past nine in the evening he was between the Crown Inn and the William the Fourth, and saw Eleanor Bull, a reputed prostitute, come from the front door of defendant's house. She then went back again. She did not come out again till a quarter to eleven, when she left the house in the company of a man.

He afterwards saw Margaret Whiteman come out of the house with several men. It was eleven o'clock when she left. He was standing near the place from half-past nine that evening. He believed they were both prostitutes. There had been a complaint made about Margaret Whiteman staying at the Two Sawyers, but she had recently taken to the William the Fourth, and Porter, the landlord of the Two Sawyers, had told witness that she was allowed to go to Jarrett's house, but not to his.

Jarrett said he did not get home till half-past eight, and went indoors after he had seen to his horse about twenty to ten. He did not see them in there then. His Worship asked him whether he knew the women were prostitutes. Jarrett said he did not.

He was fined 20s. and 11s. costs and his licence was endorsed. In default of payment it was to be one month's imprisonment. Jarrett said he thought he had better take the month, but the money was paid during the day and the defendant was released.[5]

In 1881 the William the Fourth was renamed the Kings Arms, and in 1885 it became tied to the Hodges and Ritchie Brewery of Rye.

In 1886 landlord William Mills claimed to the magistrates that he had 'lost his licence' and asked for a replacement. But it was later discovered that he had in fact pledged his licence as a form of security for a loan of £40 from the London Deposit Bank. Interestingly, the bank recognised a publican's licence as property against which they would lend money but refused to return the licence until the loan was repaid![6]

Over the next 20 years, from 1886, the image of the Kings Arms improved but not enough to save it from its final demise. In 1906 the pub was tied to Leney's of Dover for beer only. But it also sold an average of 116 gallons [527 litres] of spirits a year and was making a profit of £100 per annum. But although reprieved it was still selected for closure on the grounds that it was no longer required.

It was described by the police as 'having only one entrance which opens into the public bar; on the right of the bar is a bar parlour and a sitting room. A kitchen and scullery completes the ground floor. The upstairs accommodation consists of three bedrooms, sitting room, w.c and attic. There is a passage at the side of the house with a door in Cinque Ports Street and in this passage is a public urinal and a back door to the house opens into the passage.' Thus, the original 'long room' had been divided into smaller bars.

Three years later, in 1909, the pub was selected a second time for closure on the basis that there were three other fully licensed

Kings Arms on left and Pipemakers in the middle distance, c1900s

pubs: the Crown, the Pipemaker's and the Standard within 100 yards [91.44 metres]. This time the Kings Arms luck ran out and it was finally closed during that year. Compensation of £745 was granted to Leney's Brewery of Dover. Further compensation of £120 was granted to the last landlord, Moses Hoad, for the loss of his licence.[7]

The original building has since been pulled down and the site is now occupied by Cinque Ports Antiques.

Leney's Brewery of Dover

137

Kings Arms today

London Stout House
Ferry Road

1900

The first mention of the London Stout House occurs in about 1850 when it was known as Huggett's Beer House. Landlord Henry Huggett, originally of Peasmarsh, was a sawyer, timber merchant, and proprietor of a local timber yard. It was one of the few beer houses in Rye that we know about. To date several others are still 'hidden from history'.

Henry Huggett is first mentioned in 1842 and again in 1843 as a proprietor 'of a saw yard in Rye', when one William Brayborn was indicted for stealing his tools and his timber.[1]

Huggett's Beer House featured in the 'treating scandal' during the General Election of 1852. In the government inquiry which followed in 1853, (where Huggett's was mistakenly referred to as the Bricklayers Beer House), the inquiry showed that three days before the election, Henry Huggett provided a free dinner for 50 customers paid for by the election agent.

Considering the small size of the premises his customers must have eaten in shifts. Being a beer (only) house the wines and spirits had to be brought in and were supplied by Stephen Fryman, Wine and Spirit Merchant, and former landlord of the Dial in the High Street.

In 1864 Huggett's Beer House was owned and leased by a Mrs Barber to local brewers Messrs Chapman and Elliot (later Chapman Brothers), who subsequently became the freeholders of the property in 1878. For some unknown reason they never applied for a full licence and the premises remained a house for beer only.[2]

As far as we know Henry Huggett ran his beer house until about 1870, assisted at times by his son David, also a sawyer and an undertaker. The house became variously known as the Sawyers, the Sawyers Arms and the Two Sawyers, but by the middle of that decade it was usually referred to by locals as the Two Sawyers, after Henry and David Huggett.

In *Rye Memories* Eileen Bennett recalled the 'Rye bear story' from the later years of the century. 'A foreign looking man with a bear on a chain', she writes, 'would visit Rye and collect money in the streets. At the rear of the Two Sawyers where the bear used to put up for the night, there was a shed with strong rings in the back wall. Here the bears (sometimes there were more than one), were chained up and people in the neighbouring houses were not too happy to hear them scrapping in the night.'[3]

Another participant corroborated this story. "The Two Sawyers", stated Herbert Wright, "was a lodging house for Italian organ grinders, one man bands and dancing bears. You entered the lodgings at the back through a wooden door under the outside steps. In those days we had a lot of street performers in Rye." The steps led up to the bar on the first floor, while the taproom was at the front. The beer was stored in "a kind of underground place — an underground scullery".

In 1885 landlord George Tedham lent a 'spud' tool to a customer who was working at hop digging on a local farm. Although the landlord received some beer for the loan, the 'spud' was never returned and eventually the customer was charged with theft. Hop digging was a form of seasonal employment not to be confused with hop picking. The spud tool was also used in the fight against the ubiquitous thistle.

Radclyffe Hall in her novel: *The Sixth Beatitude*, a romantic view of local poverty first published in 1934, wrote about the downtrodden condition of some of Rye's 19th century residents, and about an occupation that many of them followed in the summer months — casual work on Romney Marsh known as 'thistle-spudding'.

The work required the digging up of thistles by hand, using an antique farm tool known as a 'spud' or 'thistle spudder', a sharp weeding hoe mounted on a long handle. In the summer months many hundreds from Rye and elsewhere went 'spudding' on the marsh.

There was thistle-spudding all over the marsh. An army of thistles, an army of spudders. A simple thing this thistle-spudding? Not at all. A most skilled and arduous business and one that seemed well nigh interminable. From end to end of a field went the spudders returning to the spot from which they had began, then forward again and always more thistles, strong, green and defiant — the pirates of the soil, brandishing boldly their many spiked spears, plunging them into the paws of dogs and into the enemy's unwary ankles ... the long handled spud with its chisel shaped blade dare not leave so much as a shoot still standing; out must come the green pirate with its roots intact, to be flung aside to die in the sunshine. No mercy, no quarter, but war to the death. Make way for the kindly grass of the marsh! Make way for the pasture that feeds the Marsh cattle.[4]

In 1892 the same landlord, George Tedham, was charged with being drunk on the premises. In his defence he admitted being drunk but only 'sensible drunk'.

'Sensible drunk', a new form of drunkenness – or at least an old form under a new name – has appeared in Rye, and it adopts the name of 'sensible'. The Two Sawyers' Inn is the abode of the respected gentleman who has unearthed this new name, for use when a man is only moderately drunk; the name of the gentleman is George Tedham, who, when charged with being drunk on his licensed premises on the 13th inst., said that he was 'sensible drunk' and that he was able to attend to his business all right. From the evidence given by Sergeant Reed and P C Willard it appeared that Tedham, on the day in question, had to hold on to tables, etc., in order that he might preserve his equilibrium. Tedham put it down to having some friends to visit him, and said that he was 66 years old and had never before appeared before any Magistrates. A moderate fine of 2s 6d was imposed, and in addition to this the costs were 14s., so that Tedham had to pay 16s 6d for getting 'sensible drunk'. In case anyone is not quite clear upon the degree of drunkenness, we may say that we understand a man to be 'sensible drunk' when he is just sensible enough to know that he is drunk.[5]

Soon after, the 'sensible drunks', bears, organ grinders and 'spudders' seem to have moved on, and the brewery attempted to create a new image with a new name, a new landlord and some new products. The new landlord and lessee was Frederick Bryant, the new name was the London Stout House, and the new product was Coombe's London Stout.

Chapman's were the local agents for Coombe's London Stout and Porter, and the new name was an attempt to promote these two beers which the pub supplied, in 'one and two gallon jars fitted with a tap' for home consumption. Selling 'take-a-way' beer prepackaged in tapped jars was, at the time, a new innovation updating the traditional Jug and Bottle trade.

When Frederick Bryant left in 1900 to become the landlord of the Union Inn, he directly employed Thomas Herbert Buckland to take over as manager of the London Stout House. An employment agreement between them stipulated that Thomas Buckland was to be paid '15 shillings weekly', (the equivalent of £50 spending power today), and be provided 'with suitable lodging at the London Stout House together with such gas as he may require. Coal to be supplied by himself. The employer will pay all rates and taxes.'

For his part Thomas Buckland was required 'to hand over all monies received, to keep a true account of the stock and to conduct the London Stout House in a fit and proper manner'. Only seven days notice to quit were required on either side.[6]

In 1908 the London Stout House became yet another victim to the 1904 Licensing Act when the police claimed 'the London Stout

House was suffering from a declining custom'. After closure total compensation of £467 was awarded and divided between the brewers and the licensee.[7]

London Stout House today

Mermaid Inn
Mermaid Street

Mermaid Street

The cellars of the Mermaid Inn date from 1156 when the original building was thought to have been built. It was rebuilt in 1420 after the French landed and set fire to the town in 1377.

The Mermaid's peak period was 1550 to 1758, and during the 18th century it was in regular use by Rye Corporation for the celebration of various events and dates in the Corporation calendar.

These included Sessions Dinners, Freemen's Dinners, Mayoring Day, the letting of the Corporation farms and the annual Herring Feast. All were recorded on Chamberlain's vouchers issued by Rye Corporation.

Chamberlain's voucher 1742 [1]

For reasons known only to the Corporation, their interest in the Mermaid as a venue for celebration came to an abrupt end in 1751. It has been suggested that this may have been due to the patronage of the smuggling fraternity. However, smugglers and smuggling were generally supported by the Rye community which makes this a doubtful theory.

Kenneth Clark in his *Short History of Rye* wrote that 'when all of the troops were withdrawn during the American War of Independence [1775–1783], smuggling on the south coast increased considerably, and Rye itself shared in the general lawlessness'.

In 1735 Gabriel Tomkins, a bailiff working for the Sheriff of Sussex, was staying at the Mermaid when he arrested Thomas Moore of Rye for an offence against the revenue laws. Moore was subsequently freed on bail. The landlord at the time was Thomas Bean. Moore, with four or five others, was able to enter the bailiff's room at the Mermaid and force him downstairs and into the street where they took from him all the bail bonds and warrants against smugglers. Tomkins was taken to the harbour and put aboard a boat but was eventually released by the commander of the Rye revenue sloop. It appears that at least one Mermaid landlord was in cahoots with the local smugglers.[2]

In 1847 local author William Holloway claimed he was 'informed some years ago by a gentleman who was born in Rye in 1740, that he remembered when the Hawkhurst gang of smugglers were at the height of their pride and insolence, to have seen them, (after successfully [having] run a cargo of goods on the sea shore) seated at the windows of this house, carousing and smoking their pipes, with their loaded pistols lying on the table before them, no magistrate daring to interfere with them.' However, he does not give a reference.[3]

Some years later in the late 19th century, travel writer Louis Jennings set down his thoughts on the Mermaid, after a visit to Rye:

The Mermaid — still I looked about me for the Mermaid Inn. I roamed up and down Mermaid Street, over the rough cobble stones, loath to give up the search.

At last I met with an ancient man, who looked as if, with a little effort of memory, he might recall the Mermaid, or perhaps be the Merman who married her.

"Ah, sir", said he with a sigh, "the inn has long been closed. How curious you should ask for it. Gone ever so long ago, sir. But" said he, "I will show you the house which was the inn; a labouring man lives in it now. It goes up three or four steps — there it is, sir." I knocked at the door, and a woman opened it — not old for a wonder.

"Can you tell me if this was the Mermaid Inn?" "Yes, but now we lives in it." And she, so far as I could judge, was not a mermaid. Presently, she offered to show me the old carvings, for which the house had a certain sort of celebrity, and I followed her without fear or trembling down a long and dark passage, and into a large room where the broad fireplace was enclosed in a framework of fine carved oak, black with age. There were carved oak panellings near it, and probably they had once gone round the entire room, but the hand of the spoiler has been there.

"Would you like to see the tiles in the old lady's room?" asked the young woman. "I should like it much", said I, "if the old lady would not object". So I went upstairs, and was shown into a room large enough to hold a hundred people. There was only one old woman in it.

"Many gentlefolks come here to see these tiles", said she, pointing to her fireplace; and indeed they were well worth seeing – fine old Dutch tiles, blue and white, going all round the chimney and hearth. Each tile was the subject of a different picture, and most of the pictures represented seafaring scenes.

Then they took me up into the attics – large, roomy apartments, with huge oaken timbers running across them; and from thence into so many rooms and closets and queer old places that I got lost, and should never have found my way out without a guide. The old house had been built to last for ever.[4]

In 1888 there was a serious fire in Mermaid Yard when the stables and some cottages were destroyed and subsequently rebuilt. The 1891 census records eight cottage households in the yard, some of which were auctioned with the Mermaid, at the George Hotel in 1894.

PUBLIC SALE OF PROPERTY.—An important sale of property was effected by Messrs. Jas. C. Vidler, Son, and Clements, at the George Hotel, Rye, on Wednesday afternoon last. There was an exceedingly large attendance of buyers, and bidding was fairly brisk generally, but very brisk over the last lot submitted. The first item on the schedule was the desirable freehold property known as the Mermaid Inn, but now forming 36 and 37, Mermaid-street, with two cottages in the rear, let at a yearly rental of £41 12s. when fully let. This lot is of great historical interest, and was sold for £410 to Miss Peel. Lot 2, which was No. 35, Mermaid-street, was not sold, but two three-roomed cottages in the rear were sold to Mr. C. Hayles for £130. Lot 3, being a portion of the stabling in Mermaid Yard, was withdrawn, but a similar lot, at present let to Mr. J. L. Deacon at a rental of £9 8s., was bought by Mr. Hayles for £120.

1894 [5]

In 1895 after a period of around 145 years the Mermaid reopened, not as an inn or public house but as a private hotel incorporating a registered club. At the first Annual General Meeting of its shareholders in 1896, the secretary reported that they 'had undoubtedly a most successful summer. We have been favoured with many artist visitors and golfers ... keeping the rooms fully occupied until late autumn.' Consequently the company paid out a dividend of 10%.[6]

Their success continued and in 1905 the 'extraordinary increase in club membership' was noted by the magistrates who had little control over clubs, which at the time were being strongly criticised by the temperance movement as 'secret drinking venues'.

This was particularly the case if a club had no apparent reason for trading other than selling alcohol. Thus, it was no coincidence that the Mermaid started describing itself as a 'golfer's club'.

However, the temperance lobby may have had a point. In 1908 the Mermaid was unsuccessfully sued by Ehrmann Bros, Wine Merchants of Finsbury Square, London, for the non-payment of a wine bill totalling £101. 0s 6d. This very large sum (in today's terms about £6,000), indicates the volume of wine consumed by club members in just 6 months![7]

For seven consecutive years, from 1925 until 1931, the Mermaid applied for a full licence but all seven applications were refused by the magistrates, some of whom were 'tee-totallers' and all of whom were influenced by the temperance issue. The application in 1931 was not helped by the fact that the manageress, Charlotte Breem, had been fined for serving someone who was not a club member, possibly a policeman incognito.

The Rye magistrates believed that granting the Mermaid a full licence would increase the total number of licences in Rye, which was against the spirit of the law. They were also lobbied and influenced by the local temperance movement in the form of Rye Baptist Church, Rye Free Church and the Salvation Army, who attended the Brewster Sessions. In 1931 after all their attempts to get a full licence the Mermaid proprietor sold up and moved on.

The Mermaid was then auctioned at the George Inn at least twice, the second time reaching only £6,500 before being withdrawn.[8]

In 1932 a letter appeared in the *Sussex Express:*

THE PASSING OF THE "MERMAID" INN.

SIR. — *It was sad to read your account in last week's paper of the fate of the Mermaid Inn. As you say, one of the most eminent historic inns in the world now stands empty and derelict. It was a part of Rye, and helped to make Rye famous. To those who have studied the question it is manifest that the continued and repeated refusal of the magistrates to grant it a licence was the cause of its ultimate downfall.*

There are many who are saying, and with some truth, that the Bench showed considerable lack of vision in this matter. It is a matter of common knowledge that the "Mermaid" was an attraction to the town and brought people to it, people moreover who returned to Rye again, perhaps repeatedly. I am at a loss to understand the motives that influenced the Bench. Was it suggested that a licence to the Inn was subversive of the cause of temperance or likely to lead to an increase of drunkenness in the town? Hardly so, surely.

One is aware of the chariness with which new licences are granted in these days, but this would not have been exactly a new licence, but the revival of an old one; further, the granting of the licence would have benefited the revenue, in a time when every added pound is needed and welcomed. It seems to me that if the licensing magistrates had taken a broader view of the question a view not unmixed with a little Rye patriotism, and granted the licence, a calamity such as has occurred would have been averted, and benefit would have accrued indirectly to the town. I have no axe to grind, nor any interest, pecuniary or otherwise, in the matter, so conclude by ascribing myself as just

A LOOKER-ON.

A few years later the Mermaid was subject to the attention of the True Temperance Association who emphasised pub improvement rather than abolition, and in the 1930s they published a brief history of the Mermaid written by local author A G Bradley. 'This brochure', he said, 'is designed to remind the public that the British Inn has its own genius, that at its best it is one of the finest of the world's social institutions, and that in connection with modern public house improvement the British tradition, rather than the foreign

Mermaid courtyard today

café type, is most worthy of being followed.' However, this was all quite erroneous being published at a time when the Mermaid remained closed without a licence.

In 1948 [9] it was granted a full licence but was not allowed to install a bar. Following financial problems it closed again in 1949. Seven years later in 1955 the bar restriction was lifted after 1,600 people signed a petition stating they had been refused a drink.[10] The lounge bar then opened and the Mermaid thus finally reverted to the status of a fully licensed premises after a period of 197 years (1758–1955).

More of the Mermaid courtyard today

Mermaid Inn sign

Oak Inn
High Street

1902

Very little information has come to light about this fishermen's beer house located on the High Street over a century ago. The earliest known date for the Oak is 1870 when Alfred Bourn was the licensee. However, as a beer house, we can be fairly certain it was in existence well before then, and possibly dated back to the Beer Act of 1830. The house was then known as the Pig and Whistle.

Pig and Whistle is a stereotypical name for the traditional English pub, but oddly enough there are or were few actual genuine pubs with this name in the country. I quote the *Dictionary of Pub Names* by Dunkling and Wright. 'When Lillywhite* examined 17,000 London pub signs in the 19th century, he was unable to find a single example of Pig and Whistle. We estimate that in the 1980s about 10 British pubs were so called.' Thus it would seem that the Pig and Whistle, Rye had an unusual name.

The *Oxford English Dictionary* gives several examples of the use of the phrase 'pigs and whistles' dating from 1681. To go to 'pigs and whistles' at one time meant 'to go to rack and ruin'. If going to pigs and whistles was going to ruin, and constantly going to the pub was also going to ruin, then pigs and whistles would be associated sooner or later with the pub. From there it would be a short step to naming a pub the Pig and Whistle, first as a nick-name, then as an official name.[1]

We can also speculate on a second theory, that the origin of the name might well have been a very local one: the Sussex Pigs of Rye Pottery! It is known that the famous Rye Pottery Sussex Pig was in use as a drinking vessel for more than 200 years. The pig was hollow and came apart. The head could be removed and would stand alone, on its snout and ears, as a cup or mug. The body of the pig set upright

*Bryant Lillywhite: 'London Signs' 1972

Rye Pottery Sussex Pig

could be used as a jug. According to the *Sussex County Magazine* it was a Rye tradition at weddings for guests to drink a whole 'hogs head' of beer in one, when toasting the bride and bridegroom. This tradition is dated to the mid-19th century when the Pig and Whistle in the High Street might have been open as a thriving beer house.

Yet another origin of the name, one favoured by bar room etymologists, is found in religious mythology. 'Pige-Washael' was once upon a time believed to be the angel's salutation to the Virgin Mary, which, in the language of the Danes meant 'Virgin Hail' or 'Health to the Maiden'.

Meanwhile back at the Oak Inn, Thomas Osborne took the licence in 1881, and sought permission of the magistrates at the Brewster Sessions to change the name 'Pig and Whistle' to the 'Oak Inn'. This change was readily agreed, but created some amusement on the bench as 'Oak Inn' was regarded to be a pretentious name for a simple beer house. However, as far as is known, Thomas Osborne never applied for a full licence and appears to have been content with beer house status.

This remained the case until the last and final landlord, George Collyer, ran the premises from 1900 to 1909. Collyer, originally from Ramsgate, took the licence of the Oak Inn five years after leaving the Royal Engineers in 1895.

The final description of the Oak Inn beer house was a sad and poignant one. When the Oak was finally referred for closure in 1909 the owners, Style and Winch Ltd of Maidstone, didn't even bother to turn up to the hearing, and the Oak Inn, one of the last beer houses in Rye, went to the wall.

The magistrates considered the closure of the Oak along with two public houses, the Kings Arms and the Queen Adelaide. This is the report in full:

THE OAK INN

The owners of the Oak Beerhouse were not represented, and the tenant, Mr C A Collyer, appeared in person.

The Superintendent's report on the house was as follows : – The Oak Beerhouse is situated in the High-street, and is two houses thrown into one. There are three entrances from High-street; one opens into the public bar, one into the bottle and jug department, and one into the private bar; and on one side of the private bar is a bar parlour, access to this being gained from the private bar. A public tap room is situate at the back of the bar, and in addition there is a kitchen and scullery on the ground floor. There is also a public entrance from the Undercliff, with a sign board above, by which access is had to the back of the house from the Salts, etc, below, through the back yard, where [there] is a w.c. and public urinal. A private entrance to same yard is gained by way of Ockman's Lane. The upstairs accommodation is eight bedrooms and a sitting-room. Lodgings are let to working-men. The nearest licensed houses are the Union Inn and the George Hotel; the former is 76 yards from the Oak, and the latter 100 yards, and the house has a frontage of 37½ feet.

Sergeant Verrion corroborated the statements in the report, and said he had no complaints to make as regard the conduct of the house because there was practically no trade. It was a house that was rarely visited by the police, because there was not very often anyone in there. The fishing class of people patronised it, but not many of these. There was accommodation for the fishing fraternity in the Union Inn. He did not consider the house was wanted. The people who lived in the immediate neighbourhood did not visit it. The house was managed during the day by Mrs Collyer, while her husband went to work.

C A Collyer, the licensee of The Oak, said he had been there nine years come June. He had had a lot of expense with his wife's illness and trying to keep a respectable house, but the people would not go there, because they were seen. It was too public. The trade might increase if the rougher class were admitted. He let for lodgings, and had ten beds. He had had eight soldiers billeted on him when they had been through. He sold a barrel and a half a week. He did not get a living by the house. If he took in all sorts of lodgers he might get a living but he took in the working class. He had got two permanent lodgers now.

THE DECISIONS

After a short retirement of the Bench, the Mayor said the licence, of the Queen Adelaide would be renewed and the King's Arms and the Oak would be referred.[2]

After being referred to the Compensation Authority, £254 was granted to the brewers Style and Winch for the loss of their beer house although they were obviously glad to be rid of it, and compensation of £60 was granted to landlord George Collyer for the loss of his licence.[3]

Style & Winch Brewery, Maidstone

Farmer Ale sold in the Oak Beer House

The Oak today

Old Bell

The Mint

The original Old Bell next door to the Staffordshire-ware house after 1899

Early records show the Old Bell to be licensed in August 1845. However, part of the building is very old having been in existence since the mid-15th century, and is quite likely to have been licensed centuries ago.

What is believed with more certainty is that the premises, at different times in the past, have been used for the covert storage of smugglers contraband. Before August 1845 the original Old Bell, or part of it, was probably a shop. Local tradition suggests that the shop and several other buildings in the street were much frequented by smugglers in the 17th century and before.

The original Old Bell was much smaller than it is today. A part of the current pub and the site of the beer patio, was a forge in the 1800s belonging to blacksmith John Manser, and was in use servicing horse drawn traffic until it was sold at the turn of the 19th century.

Old Bell Yard, then located behind the forge, was accessed via Mint Court next door. After Manser's death the forge was eventually sold to John Cooper, another blacksmith, in 1860. Cooper then sold the property to Stephen Southerden for £360 who in turn sold it, or part of it, to Henry Gasson for £100 in 1899. The big drop in price suggests that the forge was gradually becoming obsolete possibly due to competition and a decline in horse drawn traffic.[1]

1890s showing the rear of the blacksmith's forge

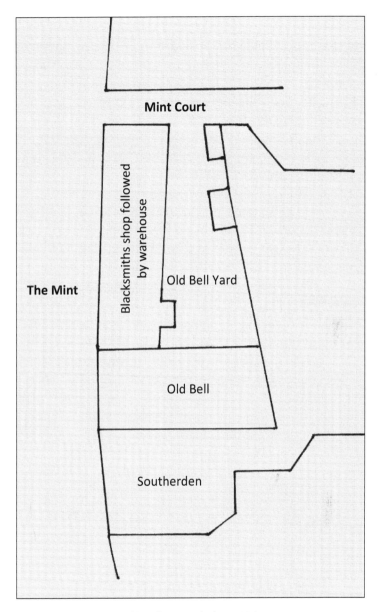

Old Bell ground plan 1899

On becoming owner of the forge, Henry Gasson, described as a Staffordshire ware dealer, demolished the building and replaced it with offices and a warehouse. The warehouse remained in situ until 1934.[2]

The pub landlord from 1890 to 1899 was Charles Fletcher, who was also the local 'Collector of District and Water Rates, Ground Rents and Inspector of Petroleum'. With the coming of the combustion engine and the need for more petrol storage facilities in the town, his main job became more important, and he finally gave up the Old Bell in 1899.

In 1906 the Old Bell was one of six pubs in Rye briefly threatened with closure. The police stated that the Old Bell, Foresters Arms, Greyhound, Borough Arms, Kings Arms and the Pipemakers were redundant and no longer required, as they estimated that Rye had one pub for every 136 people. The Old Bell and the Pipemakers are the only two of this group still open for business.[3]

From its early days the Old Bell Inn was tied to Bowen's Brewery of Rye, followed by Leney's Brewery of Dover, and then the Star Brewery of Eastbourne, who paid £600 for it in 1924.

Ten years later in 1934, the Star Brewery purchased Gasson's Staffordshire Warehouse which until then had been a separate property. Its demolition allowed them to enlarge and extend the original Old Bell by building the archway, the bell feature, the lounge bar and beer patio that we see today. Its exterior walls were rebuilt using alternate stone and brickwork, and the bell and arch were designed and constructed to form a feature spanning the corner entrance with a beer patio frontage.

Matches, sold in the 1920s, advertising the Star Brewery

This innovative and modern pub redevelopment was most probably the work of Eastbourne radical architect Andrew Ford, then employed by Eastbourne's Star Brewery designing and redesigning many of their licensed premises.

The Pipemaker's Arms in Rye, a pub also tied to the Star Brewery, is another example of a pub redesigned and rebuilt in the 1930s, as was the Carlisle on Hastings sea front with its sun lounge and roof garden. Many former Star pubs have the stamp of 1930s architecture.[4]

However, this redevelopment probably destroyed any evidence of the smuggling fraternity who used the original buildings in the 18th century. The following article by D G Southerden is quoted in full from the *Sussex County Magazine* for 1928, six years before the pub was enlarged and redeveloped.

SMUGGLERS' HOLES AT RYE

Evidences of the bygone smuggling days can be found in many of the old houses of Rye. In the days of the stage coach the inns of the various towns were halting places or destinations of those who made the journey by road, and one inn of Rye shows, or rather, did show traces of smuggling. Unfortunately the hand of the builder has destroyed or altered the evidence.

At the west end of the High Street, standing at the top of a short hill known as 'The Mint', is 'Ye Olde Bell Inn'. It is now just an ordinary public-house, and the house above it is a shop. In the eighteenth century these two houses were connected, as a doorway shows (now filled up) just inside the shop door, and the space at the back of these houses formed the inn's stable yard. That two houses, one a prosperous inn, the other a private dwelling, should be connected, is only a link in the chain of evidence.

In the room at the rear of the shop a tall recess or cupboard is built into the wall opposite to the 'Old Bell', this cupboard being seven feet high and three feet six inches wide, with two large single-panelled doors. Years ago this was a revolving cupboard, and one could step into a space immediately behind a fireplace and through a doorway into the yard. This doorway is also bricked up.

Nothing could be easier for a smuggler wishing to escape detection than to step into the cupboard, close the doors, swing the

Revolving door panels

164

revolving part round, enter and swing it back again and make his way out into the yard to another street. Also, contraband could be smuggled into the inn without difficulty.

At the top of the first flight of stairs of this house was found a large 'tubby hole' or hiding place for smuggled goods. The entrance was concealed by two carved panels shown in the photo. These panels were evidently only two of a series and their origin is unknown. Possibly they came from a church as the figures carved upon them seem to be of a religious character. Again, the builder has destroyed all this and the "tubby hole" is now built into a room and the panels have passed out of the owner's hands in recent years. I can remember the panels being in position about 1912, and, as a boy, imagined all sorts of impossible things when peering into the impenetrable blackness of the hole.

Another small hole can be found by lifting two floorboards at the top of the second flight of stairs, and yet another above a doorway in the same room as the revolving cupboard. There must be many such hiding places in the old houses of Rye, some perhaps destroyed, others, perhaps, never yet discovered.[5]

1930s

The cupboard and revolving door mentioned in the article are believed to be in the British Museum. Other historic features in situ or bricked up, apparently include various tunnels and a carved Tudor Rose in the former public bar, said to commemorate the visit to Rye by Elizabeth 1st in 1573. There was also a tunnel leading to the cellars of the Mermaid Inn, nearby.

It is thought that the name Old Bell originates from 1377 when the French raided the town, stole the bells of St Mary's Church, and devastated the town by fire. Men from Rye and Winchelsea responded in the following year, 1378, when they set sail for the French coast. After much looting, pillage and burning, they returned with the bells and other loot stolen the year before. One of the bells was later hung in Watchbell Street to warn of subsequent French attacks.

Old Bell today

Pipemaker's Arms
Wish Ward

c1900

In 1778 Thomas Lamb sold four properties, on and adjoining the site of the current Pipemaker's Arms, for £180, to a bricklayer called James Honiss. Two of these properties were cottages, the third had been a herring deeze and the fourth was an adjoining shop. These four properties had various owners until about 1806 when they were purchased by Thomas Gosley, Yeoman, of Rye.[1] By 1811 Gosley had demolished the shop and replaced it with a third cottage.

Richard Cogger, formerly a stable keeper, became the tenant of one of the cottages which later became the Pipemaker's Arms, and opened it as a beer house in, it is believed, 1830. In 1832 he petitioned the magistrates for a full licence:

I Richard Cogger, retailer of beer, now residing in the Ancient Town aforesaid and for six months past having resided in the Ancient Town do hereby give notice that it is my intention to apply at the next General Annual Licensing Meeting to be holden at the Ancient Town aforesaid on the fifth day of September now next ensuing, for a license to sell ... liquors by retail to be drunk and consumed in the house ... belonging and situate near the Strandgate in the Ancient Town aforesaid and which (were in the ownership of) Thomas Gosley deceased. And intend to keep as a common Inn, alehouse and victualling house.
Signed: Richard Cogger.
1832 [2]

However, before the licensing magistrates could consider the application Richard Cogger was indicted for keeping a 'disorderly house', and any possibility of a full licence disappeared.

Richard Cogger of the Parish of Rye...retailer of beer, on the 23/4/1832 and diverse other days and times ...did keep and maintain ...a certain, common, ill governed and disorderly house ... and in his house ... said men and women ... at unlawful times in the night and in the day ...remained drinking, tippling, whoring and misbehaving themselves unlawfully ... against the peace of our said Lord, the King, his Crown and Dignity.
Signed: Thomas Leaver
      Robert Daniel
      George Gammon.   Jurors.[3]

The word 'guilty' was pencilled in underneath.

The house that became the Pipemaker's Arms and the three cottages next door were sold together in 1834. It is known that a beer house on or near this site was tenanted by Ann Cogger in 1838. She was most probably the wife or widow of Richard Cogger, and her beer house probably became the Pipemaker's Arms around that date.

Charles Bourne was landlord during the 'treating scandal' of the 1852 election, and was a significant witness in the subsequent Parliamentary Inquiry. Bourne claimed he 'had received a gift of some beer' from the Aylward Brewery, value 60s [£175 in today's terms], and was ordered 'to give it away' in the run up to the election. He also provided a free supper for 24 customers 'upstairs and down', with wine and spirits supplied by Stephen Fryman.[4]

Ten years later, in 1862, the same Charles Bourne and three of his customers were charged with 'unlawfully and maliciously by diverse false pretences and subtle devices' of obtaining £11. 5s. [about £485 today], from another customer by cheating at cards and dominoes. It was alleged they did this by signalling to each other by putting a thumb up for a double six, a fore finger for a double five, a second finger for a double four and so on.

They were apparently gambling for a period of 14 hours from midday to 2am in the morning! They played dominoes for '3d a corner' and a pint of porter. Cards were played for sovereigns and a pot of porter was drunk every 'four handed game'. The beer score came to 28 pots. William Bourn and the three customers were bailed, except for one who absconded, and sent for trial.[5]

By 1882 the Pipemakers was tied to Bowen's Eagle Brewery of Rye, and by 1890 the property was tied to the Alfred Leney brewery of Dover.

In 1892 meanwhile, the three cottages next door were pulled down and replaced by the Mission Room of the Good Shepherd which, as can be imagined, did not make for an amicable, relationship between the pub and its neighbours. Intervention by local temperance campaigners only 'poured fat on the fire', and relations between the Pipemakers and the Mission Room, in the final years of the 19th century and before the First World War, were often fractious.

In 1896 the licence was transferred to George Coleburne with advice from the magistrates to: "Keep your eyes open for your customers. I don't doubt you will have any difficulty getting them, but you might have difficulty getting rid of them."

Eight years later in 1904 the 'Pipemakers' was briefly threatened with closure under the 1904 Licensing Act. But although the pub was reprieved this action led to much rumour in the Wish Street community that the 'Pipes' days were numbered. It was reported that long time landlord Thomas Martin was irritated with 'the local tittle-tattle; that the pub would close and that the neighbours would be glad when it did so'. Within this atmosphere things came to a head in 1911.

A passageway or 'twitten' which ran between the Pipemakers and the Mission Room was used by pub customers to access the pub toilet at the rear of the building. In 1911, the toilet and the customers who used it, were the subject of a complaint by the Mission Room and other neighbours. After a police investigation Leney's brewery was instructed to improve the toilets although they claimed to have 'reconstructed the house a short while ago'. The problem was partially resolved when a new toilet was built away from the Mission Room and the passageway.

However, following this, Thomas Martin was convicted and fined for assaulting a temperance user of the Mission Room when its chimney started belching smoke into the pub and into his sitting room.[6]

By 1930 the Pipemakers was tied to the Star Brewery of Eastbourne who were responsible for its redevelopment. Clifford Bloomfield writing in *Rye Memories* in 2000 said that: 'In 1931 the

Extended bar with bas relief sign

Pipemakers was all but rebuilt except for the original building, which now stands at the centre of the present building. Car and coach parking was provided with a second entrance off the Strand. Across this entrance there was a new vehicular lych-gate with a roof high enough to accommodate visiting coaches. (The developers were certainly looking to the future.) It consisted of a tall black oak frame supporting a four gabled roof of tiles.'[7] This innovative 1930s development was, like the Old Bell, probably designed by Star Brewery architect Andrew Ford. However, the distinctive bas relief sign of two pipemakers is of a later date.

The car park sustained bomb damage in the Second World War when the adjacent Havelock Villas were destroyed in 1943. The Pipemakers itself suffered from bomb blast but the core of the pub was untouched. The lych-gate was finally demolished in 1987 when further development took place.

The car park was also used by bikers who have visited Rye for many years. The first attempt to form a Rye Motorcycle Club took place at the Pipemakers in 1925. After the war they came in increasing numbers and still come on the 'Rye run' today.[8]

RYE MOTOR CYCLE CLUB.—A meeting was held at the Pipemakers' Arms on Thursday, with the object of forming a club for motor cyclists for Rye and district. The meeting was not so well attended as was hoped, owing, no doubt, partly to the inclement weather, and partly to the short notice given, and it was decided to hold another meeting on Thursday, December 10th. All those interested are heartily invited to attend.

1925

The Pipemakers unusual name may have come from the Apps family of pipemakers in the early 19th century (see Bedford Arms), or alternatively might relate to the heraldic arms of the Pipemaker's Guild. From around 1966 until 1972 the pub was known as 'Ye Olde Pipemakers Arms'. Today it is referred to simply as the 'Pipes'.

Along with some other Rye buildings, the Pipemaker's Arms and its bas relief sign were photographed by Paul Berkshire for English Heritage in 1993.

Ye Olde Pipemaker's Arms

AND

Wish House Tea Gardens
Rye

Charabanc and Motor Car Park.

LUNCHEONS and TEAS

PARTIES CATERED FOR

Board Residence

Telephone: Proprietors:
Rye 167.   Mr. C. C. Killick and Mrs. Workman.

1930s

Pipemaker's Arms today

"KENT'S BEST" Rhymes

No: 25

THERE WAS A YOUNG FELLOW OF RYE,
WHO KNITTED A WONDERFUL TIE.
ON THE FRONT WAS HIS CREST—
A GLASS OF "KENT'S BEST",
THE FINEST BREW MONEY
CAN BUY!

"Kent's Best"

A FINE PICK-ME-UP

GEORGE BEER & RIGDEN, LTD., FAVERSHAM.

Queen Adelaide
Ferry Road

1950s

The Queen Adelaide was first opened in the early 1830s by the Albion Brewery of Rye. The exact year of opening is unknown but a comment by a brewery agent many years later recalled 'the old established character of this house which has existed since the time of William IV' (1830–1837).

The first landlord, Alexander Sinclair, was a tailor who ran the pub as a secondary occupation. As early as 1837 the Albion Benefit Society was formed here, initially with 35 members but grew in size over the years. (See Bedford Arms.)

In 1840 landlord James Phillips was issued with a distress warrant by Thomas and Charles Aylward of the Albion Brewery. The warrant was presumably for debts or money owed to the brewery. Among goods seized was a set of 'nine quoits' and the game of bat and trap. (See Ypres Castle.)[1]

From the 1850s and particularly after the opening of Rye railway station, the Queen Adelaide was a favoured port of call for hop pickers, who used the pub as a lodging house in the months of September and October, and sometimes into November. Some of the many hundreds of hoppers from nearby farms crowded its bars in the evenings.

By mid-century the Queen Adelaide, the Bedford, the Jolly Sailor, the Ship, the Two Sawyers et al, were part of an established 'hoppers' tradition, and consequently, for many years, these pubs were considered a headache by the police. The 'hoppers' presence in Rye and the surrounding countryside created much comment in the local press. In 1873 hoppers lodging here were charged with fishing in the Tillingham Channel without a licence, and with 'trespassing in search of conies' — poaching rabbits in the nearby fields.

At other times of the year customers included employees of the nearby railway yards, and gardeners from the many allotments in the area.

In September 1862, a Coroner's Inquest was held at the Queen Adelaide, into the death by drowning of a 16 year-old youth in the Tillingham Channel. The young man's body was laid out in the Adelaide for inspection, and for this reason, when the inquest was over the jurors removed to another pub for refreshment.[2]

In 1864 landlord William Warren was cautioned for harbouring 'persons of notorious bad character'. In particular he was cautioned for allowing a young female servant working in the pub, to fraternise with an army deserter who was lodging there.

At this time hours were long, and pubs were only legally obliged to close between 1 am and 4 am, but 'bona fide travellers' and lodgers could be served at anytime. The landlord admitted he 'left the door open at night for travellers who sometimes arrived late and served themselves'! When challenged about this he asked: "Can I draw beer for them?" The magistrate declined to give advice but told him: "You are not allowed to let them sit down!" In spite of his mistakes William Warren was landlord for the next 35 years until 1899.[3]

In 1902 Colour-Sergeant Edward Craig became landlord on his retirement from the Volunteers, and was immediately welcomed to the pub with a:

VOLUNTEER SMOKER AND PRESENTATION
EX-SERGT-INSTRUCTOR CRAIG'S RETIREMENT

On Saturday evening last an enjoyable smoking concert was held at the Queen Adelaide, during which an interesting presentation was made to the Host, ex-Colour-Sergt.-Instructor E.W. Craig, by members of the 'E' Company, 1st C P R V [Cinque Ports Rifle Volunteers]. There was a good attendance, Mr Twort presiding. A capital musical programme was submitted the contributors including Messrs. Neeves, Bennett, Batchelor, Summers, Boreham, E. Gasson, Weller, and Fairhall, the latter accompanying.

The Chairman, in presenting Colour-Sergeant Craig with a handsome thermometer and barometer on behalf of the Volunteers of the 'E' Company, alluded to the excellent qualities of Mr. Craig. He remarked that a man who had been in the ranks knew what the men wanted. Sergeant Craig had for many years been a leader of the Volunteers in the town, and he had been of great assistance to the Company at Camp at drilling, and also as regards the Armoury Club. Previous to his connection with the Company he had served his country well in India, and been on active service. He had great pleasure in asking Sergeant Craig to accept that memento from his friends of the 'E' Company. (Applause).

Ex-Colour-Sergeant-Instructor Craig, in returning thanks, remarked that since he had been connected with the Company, nearly eight years, the number of recruits he had passed through the Company came to nearly 200. He had always done his utmost to keep the men together in drill and in social matters, and he could not tell them how pleased he was to receive this souvenir as an appreciation of the little he had done for them. It would remind him of the happy times they had had, and he would be pleased to do anything he could at any time for the Volunteers. (Hear, hear.) He had received presents previously from the outlying sections, which he treasured as he would theirs. (Applause.)

The Sergeant's health was heartily drunk, with musical honours.[4]

Craig's record and military status proved useful six years later when the pub was threatened with closure in 1908. The magistrates were given the following information: 'The Queen Adelaide is situated close to the railway in Ferry Road. There are four entrances to the house, one into the public bar, one into the bottle and jug, one into the bar-parlour and the other into a passage leading to the smoking room. There are six bedrooms, a kitchen, scullery and cellar under the bar. A public urinal is situated in the yard at the back and a backdoor leads into the house from the yard. The frontage of this triangular house in ferry Road is 32 feet [9.75m], in Tillingham Lane 38 feet [11.58m], and the corner is 21 feet [6.4m].'

'The house is the only one in Rye belonging to the Ash Brewery of Canterbury. In 1906 there were 95 barrels and 696 dozen bottles of beer sold, making a total of 128 barrels, and in 1908 134 barrels.'

'He also lets rooms for lodgings and is a regular servant of the Crown, billeting on one occasion four men and on another three. There is an allotment garden nearby and the Queen Adelaide is the nearest house to the Railway Yard the employees of which come to the house for bread and cheese and refreshment.'

The court was also told: 'It has only had three landlords in 48 years and it is remarkable that the police have nothing to say about the trade being done.' The pub was easily reprieved.[5]

In 1911 the property was altered. This time the partition between the parlour and the kitchen was removed making the parlour bigger, and the tap room was converted into a new kitchen. On approving the plans the magistrate remarked that "tap rooms were practically useless in public houses these days". The converted parlour then became a new club room which was officially opened with a 'smoker'.

On the outbreak of the First World War, Sergeant Craig was still active in the Volunteers:

RECRUITING IN RYE AND DISTRICT

During the past few days many young men of Rye who have joined the colours returned home on a visit to their friends and relations, and in all instances they were heard to express their eagerness to return again to their duty.

We are sure that we are only expressing the sentiments of our townspeople when we say that everybody is proud of them. It is also very gratifying to note that the past week has seen a considerable increase in the number of recruits who have joined Lord Kitchener's Army. Many have responded willingly to assist in any way to help their country at this period of vital importance, and by these actions they have earned the heartiest regard of those they have left behind.

On Thursday Colour-Sergeant Craig had the pleasure of conveying a batch of 21 recruits obtained from Rye and the various districts to Hastings.[6]

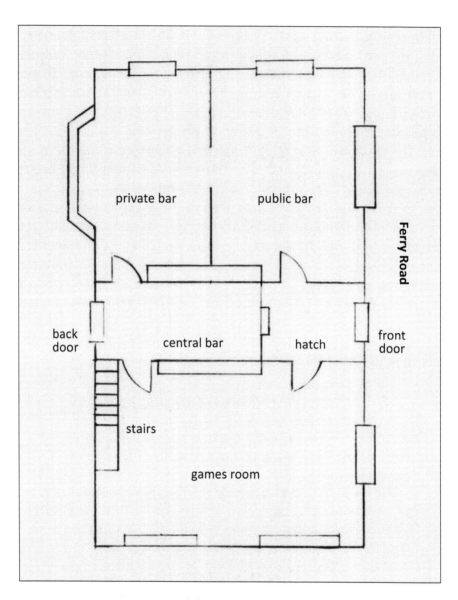

private bar

public bar

Ferry Road

back
door

central bar

hatch

front
door

stairs

games room

Queen Adelaide ground plan 1934.

That was in 1914. In 1916 Edward Craig was called up himself and was away for nearly two years. During this time his wife, Emma Craig ran the pub. On his return Edward Craig remained landlord until 1925, when he underwent an operation and was hospitalised. Emma Craig took over again and 'was the only female licensee in Rye' in 1926. Edward Craig never returned as landlord and Emma Craig continued until 1933.

Among her achievements were the three benefit clubs then operating from the pub. These were two Slate Clubs; one for men and one for women, and the Adelaide Premier Birthday Club, a basic savings club which had a staggering 785 members who in 1926, each received 8s 9d (about £15 today) share out. The Slate Clubs also had another two hundred members each!

Initially tied to the Albion Brewery of Rye the Queen Adelaide was later acquired by the Ash Brewery of Canterbury and indeed was the only Ash pub in Rye. It was later tied to Whitbreads and then to Courage.

Ash Brewery of Canterbury

QUEEN ADELAIDE
Rye

In 1949 the Adelaide sign was included in Whitbread's miniature inn sign series, one of only two in Rye.[7]

Queen Adelaide today

Queens Head
Landgate

c1895

The earliest known date for the Queens Head is 1722 when it was called the Two Brewers. A landlord of the Two Brewers in the 1760s was Richard Breeds, son of the infamous John Breeds formerly of the Flushing Inn.

Chamberlain's vouchers were issued to various landlords from at least 1745 until 1862. In 1746 landlady Elizabeth Gray was granted a payment of 6s 8d 'for licker for the ringers', and again in 1749 'for ringing on the Corporation'. In the following year a large payment of 19s 6d was made 'for the masons, carpenters and carriers' working nearby.[1]

The Two Brewers changed its name to the Queens Head in 1780, and in 1789 ownership was transferred from landlord John Pilcher, a local customs officer, to Thomas Simmonds of Canterbury.

Simmonds owned the pub until 1803 when he sold it to John Norley who was landlord during the Napoleonic Wars; a turbulent time from 1800 to 1815. In 1817 a dispute arose between John Norley and his neighbour Thomas Harrison, a wool dealer. It followed a disagreement about the ownership of a passageway or 'twitten' running from Landgate to Fishmarket Road known as Little London. Both men claimed Little London – or a portion of it – as part of their freehold. The passageway was situated at the rear and to the side of the pub, and was the location of a pub 'playground' containing a skittle alley and quoits pitch.[2]

Other premises at the rear were used as a barrack room for soldiers during the Napoleonic Wars, and also as a sty for John Norley's pigs. By the mid-19th century Little London was a busy alleyway with slum cottages, acting as a rear entrance to the pub yard and stables.

Jeremiah Smith, the mayor of Rye, had some interest in the Queens Head, when in 1848 he and Charles French were entrusted with the sale of the estate of William Norley. Four years later Jeremiah Smith was convicted of perjury in the 1852 general election.[3]

The lease of the property and the premises behind, were purchased by Francis Norley in 1849, who sub-let the warehouse and a second building, a blacksmiths shop, to Thomas Ditton.

In 1856 the Queens Head, together with a cottage, yards and buildings, was sold for £330 to Henry Gibbs, a brewer of Stourmouth,

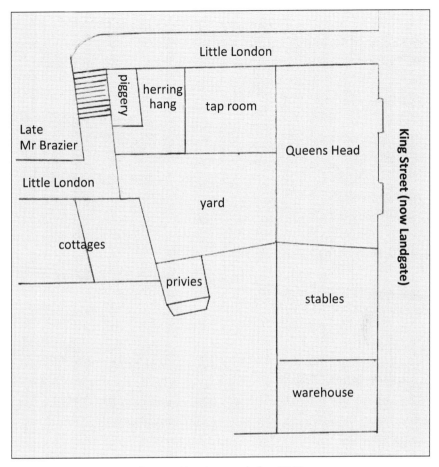

Queens Head ground plan 1843

Wingham in Kent. This was probably the end of the Queens Head as a free house.[4]

Around this time the pub provided a number of community services to the poor population of Landgate, including a cooperative coal club providing fuel to members in Landgate and Rope Walk. The Landgate Coal Club, met here to enrol members, collect funds, and to allocate and distribute coal purchased by the club, which was delivered to Rye by boat. Another similar club was the Economic Coal Club.[5]

The Rye Literary, Debating and Elocution Society also met here, and in May 1868 held their presentation dinner 'to end the season'.

In 1864 the first annual dinner of platelayers, fettlers and navvies working on the South Eastern Railway, was served by the Queens Head in a marquee on the Salts at the rear of the Bedford Arms.

THE QUEENS HEAD HARMONIC SOCIETY

The annual supper of the members of this society was held at Queens Head Inn on Tuesday evening when about 50 sat down to an excellent repast provided by host W Elliot, presided over by Mr F Fuller, supported by several other gentlemen, Mr T Wraight occupying the vice-chair. The band of the Artillery Volunteers was in attendance and contributed to the harmony of the evening, which was interspersed after supper with toast and song. A large number of visitors joined the company during the latter part of the evening which was very pleasantly spent. The expenses of the supper are met by a small weekly subscription of the members during the winter months, and the financial statement which was presented by the secretary Mr Wm. Bourne, showed a balance in hand of 9s 7d. 1875 [6]

In the 1860s, Gala Day dinners were held at the Red Lion in a marquee on the Bowling Green Arbour; at the Cinque Ports Arms in a marquee in the Rose Garden; in the Long Room at the London Trader; in the Crown, and in a marquee on the Salts by the Queens Head. The Gala Day celebrations, always in July, continued into the 1870s when interest in Gala Day by the friendly societies started to wane. At this point a smaller number of members of several societies were jointly accommodated in a booth on the Salts by landlord William Elliot. By 1878 Gala Day was almost finished as far as the procession was concerned but the dinners continued for a few years more. Another popular entertainment was dancing, particularly the quadrille danced in sets of four couples, and both Quadrille Balls and classes were held here.

Landlord William Elliot purchased the Cinque Port's Arms for £2,000 in 1882, and in 1884 gave up the Queens Head licence after 26 years. He seems to have been the last individual owner of the Queens Head before he sold it to the Style Brewery of Maidstone. The Queens Head then became a tied pub.

At the end of the century the pub was used by several organisations. The Phoenix Lodge of the Odd Fellow's re-formed here in 1893; the Rye Philanthropic Society was formed here in 1896 as was the Rye branch of the Amalgamated Society of Railway Servants in 1900, and a slate club in 1902. The Court Harold continued with 400 members until 1888, and the Rye Goal Running Club was based here in 1898.

Goal Running was a sport peculiar to East Kent and the Weald, requiring no special equipment or pitch and Rye matches were played barefoot on the Salts by teams of 10. Goal Running was an organised version of the game of tag seen in school playgrounds in which players of one team tried to evade a 'stroke' or 'touch' from members of the opposing team as they ran round the course.

GOAL RUNNING CLUB SMOKER

The Rye Goal Running Club finished up its first season, which has been so very successful, with a smoking concert at the Queen's Head Hotel, on Monday evening. There was a good attendance, and the chair was taken by Mr J Adams who, in proposing 'Success to the Rye Goal Running Club', said he must compliment the members upon having introduced into Sussex a game which, for the most part, has been confined heretofore to Kent. For their first season they had a record of eight matches played, four lost, two drawn, and two won, which he took as a good augury of what might be expected from them. As to their finances, those were in an exceedingly good condition, there being nearly £3 in hand, and as to membership, they had an enrolment of about 30. (Applause.)

He hoped next year that number would be very much increased. Goal running was capital exercise for those who took part in it, and amused the public, and was gaining a firm hold upon them. As Chairman of the Rye Regatta, he must thank the Club for their efforts to amuse the public that day. Five years ago no one would have thought that football could have made such progress in Rye as it had, and therefore he looked forward to the day when they would see goal running as popular as football was now.

Mr Arter, the captain, replied, urging upon the members to work well together, and spoke with great hopefulness of next season. Other toasts were given, and altogether, a pleasant evening was spent in harmony.[7]

RULES OF GOAL RUNNING

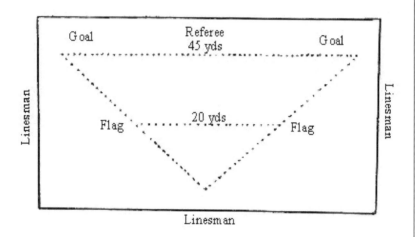

1.—30 yards from each goal a flag shall be placed, and every player who runs round his opponents' flag, and returns home to his goal uncaught, shall score a Point. Ten Points to equal one Stroke. Flags to be 20 yards apart.

2.—Forty Minutes shall be the duration of each Run. The Referee to call time at the expiration of 20 minutes, when each Club shall cross over.

3.—That the Captains shall settle the question as to whether the ground or the weather is fit for play. But if they disagree the Referee shall decide.

4.—No fresh player shall be allowed to join in the Run at half-time who has not run in the first half.

5.—Kicking Strokes shall not be counted.

6.—Every Runner must go round his own Flag before he starts from home.

7.—The Referee to mark the Stroke caught on a blackboard, and send out the side winning the Stroke.

8.—A player who has properly run round the flag, and is on his way home to his goal, shall have his Point counted even if a Stroke is caught at the same time.

Many of these organisations went into abeyance with the onset of the First World War and the pub hosted new customers. During the War the magistrates, at the request of the military, agreed that all Rye pubs should close at 9pm. But in 1916, a century after the Napoleonic Wars when the pub was previously in use by the military, the coach house and other premises attached to the Queens Head were commandeered by the military authorities once again, this time as a canteen. Their intention was to serve beer and food to the troops but the magistrates were opposed: 'We cannot vote for the military having greater facilities than the civil population', they said, and it was stopped.[8]

Following the severe restrictions of the First World War, the pub followed a much quieter life between the Wars. At some point, probably in the 1930s, the Queens Head was used as a meeting place by a group of Bonfire Boys. Which group or groups is unknown but it is most likely that a group moved here from the Railway. A plaque of the 'Rye and District Bonfire Society' adorns the front wall and shows a traditional burning boat.

Queens Head today

Red Lion
Lion Street

1860s

There are two prominent historical facts about the Red Lion. One is that it had an active relationship with its neighbours; the Town Hall, St Mary's Church and Market Street, and secondly that it was a pub or ale house dating from the middle of the Reformation (1550–1660).

As with all churches in the 16th century, nearby St Mary's was a centre of social and community activity. Pageants, processions, plays, harvest dinners, dancing, music, games and beer (church ales, bid ales and Scott ales), were all to be found within the church precincts. But under the pressure of the Protestant Ascendancy these activities were suppressed, and in this environment inns and alehouses blossomed as they inherited and took over these former church activities.

Many a parish church had a Church House on its boundary but outside its sanctity where these activities continued. Over time many church houses became licensed premises, and the Red Lion, which closely fits this pattern, most likely evolved in the same way. According to custom vestry meetings were held in the church to decide parochial matters, and then adjourned to the Red Lion.

The Red Lion also had an affiliation with the Town Hall opposite, and the pub was often used for Coroner's Inquests and to provide hospitality for jurors. Last but not least the open space known as Red Lion Yard at the back of the building is thought to have been the site of the original market.

Chamberlain's vouchers, issued by the Town Hall for the payment of victuals for various Red Lion customers, started in 1710. A noted voucher was one issued in 1743, 'for a splendid dinner for forty gentlemen and twenty-five servants at a cost of £14.10s 11d' [£14.54].[1]

Again on March 17th of the same year a Coroner's Jury was allowed 16s 8d [86p] 'for licker', and a second voucher for 2s [10p] worth of 'licker for the doctors', after the execution of John Breeds. It is assumed that the doctors had carried out a medical examination of the body. Payments were made to the Red Lion until 1862, just 10 years before its final demise.

In the mid 18th century a local author recorded the notorious Hawkhurst Gang of smugglers, 'well armed and laden with prohibited goods' sitting in the back bar of the Red Lion, coming out into the street, 'firing their pistols in the air to intimidate the inhabitants; and observing one James Marshall, a young man too curious of their behaviour, carry'd him off, and he has not been heard of since.'[2]

This is to acquaint the Public,

THAT THOMAS EDWARDS, Peruke-Maker, at Winchelfea in Suffex, hath taken the RED LYON INN in Rye, where the beft of Accommodations, both for Man and Horfe, will be provided for thofe who fhall pleafe to favour him with their Commands, and their Kindnefs gratefully acknowledged, by Their moft obedient humble Servant,

THOMAS EDWARDS.

Note, There will be an Ordinary every Saturday, for the Convenience of Gentlemen, Farmers, and others.

1756 [3]

To be fold by AUCTION,

At Thomas Woollett's, at the Red Lion, at Rye, and not at the Swan at Hafting, as mentioned before,

SEVEN Thoufand Gallons of fine French Brandy; 2500 Gallons of French Wines, of different Kinds; 64 Hundred Weight of Caftile or Venice Soap; 1000 Bottles of Hungary Water; 24 Casks of Anchovies; 24 Hundred weight of Cork; and 15 Hundred Weight of Aleppo Galls*; all warranted neat and exceeding good, without any Adulteration, having never been in any Merchant's Cuftody, and are French Prize Goods just landed out of a neutral Ship, lately taken by the Hawk Privateer of Hafting, John Grayling, Commander, and will be put up in small Lots, for the Benefit of Gentlemen and Ladies in the Country.

The Sale to begin at Ten o'Clock precifely, on Account of the Number of Lots.

To be viewed the Day before, and at the Sale.

1758 [4]

*[Aleppo Galls: a nut like growth produced by wasps on oak trees in Asia. Used in Britain in the 18th century for medicine and in tanning.]

In 1756 Thomas Edwards of Winchelsea, a 'peruke maker' or wig maker and barber, became landlord and started supplying wigs to his customers. The term 'big-wig' stems from this period. But this venture was not a great success and eighteen months later the Red Lion was auctioned and re-let.[5]

The auction included the gardens, stables, yards and seven acres of pasture land. 'The Red Lion is well tenanted and let on a lease', claimed the auctioneer. Real estate was not the only thing up for auction. Works of art taken from a French ship during the Seven Years War [1756-1763]; sea-going vessels including cutters and privateers; 'a gentlemen's library' and smuggler's contraband; all went under the auctioneer's hammer.

After the George and the Mermaid, the Red Lion has been described as Rye's 'third major inn'. The technical and legal definition of an inn was a licensed premises catering for travellers. With only four bedrooms the Red Lion was not an inn but a first class alehouse, with considerable status as a coaching house, excise office, posting house and auction room. Importantly, most if not all of the town's major events are connected with the history of the Red Lion.

bill head 1793

BOLT-IN-TUN

ROYAL MAIL & COACH ESTABLISHMENT,

Sussex Tavern and Family Hotel,

FLEET STREET, LONDON.

Royal Mails.

PORTSMOUTH & ISLE of WIGHT, With a Branch to Chichester, Bognor, & Petworth.

HASTINGS & TUNBRIDGE WELLS, With a Branch to Rye and Hawkhurst.

Every Evening .... at Half-past Seven o'Clock.

Fast Coaches.

	Morning	Afternoon
ABERYSTWITH, Kington, Penybont, and Rhayader	7	4
ALRESFORD, Alton, and Farnham	8	
BATH, Melksham, Devizes, Marlborough, and Hungerford	7	¼ to 7
BIRMINGHAM, Stratford-on-Avon, Shipston, and Woodstock	7	
BLACKWATER, Sandhurst (Royal Military College,) Egham, and Staines		3
BRISTOL, Clifton, Bath, Devizes, and Newbury	7	¼ to 7
BRIGHTON, Reigate, and Crawley	¼ past 8 ¼ past 10	
CHELTENHAM, Witney, and Oxford	7 & ¼ to 8	¼ past 4
CHICHESTER, Midhurst, Haslemere, Petworth, and Godalming	9	¼ past 7
CHERTSEY, Shepperton, Halliford, Sunbury, and Hampton	¼ past 8	¼ past 4
CAERMARTHEN, Llandilo, Llandovery, Brecon, and Crickowell	7	4
DOVER, Deal, Canterbury, Sittingbourne, and Rochester	9	¼ past 6
ESHER, Claremont, Ditton, and Kingston	8 & 9	¼ past 3
EXETER, Cullompton, Wellington, Bridgwater, Taunton, and Wells	7	¼ to 7
FROME, Trowbridge, and Devizes	7	
GLOUCESTER, Cheltenham, Northleach, Burford, Witney, and Oxford *(In direct communication with Coaches for all parts of South Wales.)*	7 & ¼ to 8	¼ past 4
GODALMING, Guildford, Ripley, Cobham, and Esher	8 & 9	¼ to 3
HAMPTON COURT, Hampton, Twickenham, and Richmond	8 & ¼ p. 10	¼ past 3 ¼ past 6

	Morning	Afternoon
HEREFORD, Ross, Gloucester, Cheltenham, and Oxford	¼ to 7	¼ past 4
HASTINGS, Battle, Robertsbridge, Flimwell, and Tunbridge	10	¼ past 7
MARGATE and Ramsgate	9	¼ past 6
MONMOUTH, Whitchurch, and Ross	7	4
OXFORD	7 & 8	4
PORTSMOUTH, Horndean, Petersfield, Liphook, and Godalming	¼ past 8	2 ¼ past 7
READING, Wokingham, Bracknell, and Virginia Water	¼ past 11	4
RYE, Northiam, Sandhurst, Hawkhurst, and Lamberhurst	11	¼ past 7
SHREWSBURY, Bridgnorth, and Kidderminster	7	4
SOUTHAMPTON, Winchester, Alton, Farnham, and Guildford	¼ past 8	
St. LEONARDS and Hastings	10	¼ past 7
SEVEN OAKS and Riverhead	10 & 11	¼ past 3
SWANSEA, Neath, Cowbridge, Cardiff, Newport, and Chepstow	7	4
TUNBRIDGE WELLS, Tunbridge, and Seven Oaks	10	¼ past 2 ¼ past 7
WARMINSTER, Trowbridge, and Devizes	7	
WEYBRIDGE, Oatlands, Walton, Moulsey, and Hampton Court		¼ past 3
WINCHESTER and Farnham	8	
WINDSOR, Eton, and Slough (Patronized by Her Majesty.)	¼ past 8 ¼ past 9	¼ past 2 4
WORCESTER and Tewkesbury	7	4
WALLINGFORD and Henley	8	

ROBERT GRAY & CO. Proprietors.

Every information relative to the different **STEAM PACKETS** from

BRISTOL .... to Cork, Waterford, Swansea, Ilfracomb, Haverfordwest, and Tenby.

PORTSMOUTH .... to the Isle of Wight, Torquay, Plymouth, and Falmouth.

SOUTHAMPTON .... to the Isle of Wight, Guernsey, Jersey, St. Maloes, Havre de Grace, France, and Italy.

☞ **NOTICE.**—No Parcel, or Passenger's Luggage, will be accounted for above the Value of **Ten Pounds** unless entered as such, and Insurance paid accordingly.

In 1788 the first stage coach left for London from here. The Street Directory informs: 'A coach sets out from the Red Lion every Tuesday and Friday morning at 5 o'clock and arrives at the Bolt in Tun, Fleet Street, London the same day; from whence on the same morning a coach sets out and arrives at Rye the same evening. Fare nineteen shillings.'[6]

In the 1820s the Red Lion was a centre for the local Reform Movement and the 'Men of Rye'. It was also a busy meeting place for the Lodges of the Foresters Friendly Society.

Town hall opposite the Red Lion c1825

There are no known architect's plans of the Red Lion and only one photograph showing a corner of the building, but valuations made in 1867 and 1868 tell us that the Red Lion was a smallish, two storey building of 12 rooms with six acres of grounds at the rear. These grounds contained Red Lion yard, the terminus for mail and passenger coaches accessed via a small roadway, about 20 metres wide, from Lion Street.

Both valuations inform us that the Red Lion had two parlours, a bar, commercial room, club room, bagatelle room, kitchen, pantry and larder on the ground floor, with four bedrooms and a laundry on the first floor.

The large open space at the rear contained a coach house, three stables, a skittle alley, pig pound, cookery outhouse and a 'bowling green arbour'. The yard was also the location of the Old Tap Room, used by coachmen and ostlers from the stables.[7] A game played in the parlour was the Wheel of Fortune, almost certainly another name for Spinning Jenny or Twister. (See the Forester's Arms.)

Four years later in 1872 the life of the Red Lion came to a drastic end when it was demolished by a:

DESTRUCTIVE FIRE IN RYE

One of the largest and most destructive fires that have happened in Rye for many years broke out early yesterday morning at the Red Lion Inn, Lion-street, the property of the Meryon family, and all that remains of the entire building is a heap of smouldering ruins.

The fire appears to have originated in the bar of the Lion, and must have been burning some time before it was discovered. The occupants, Mr Frank Hemmings, with his wife and child, and servant, were sleeping in the back part of the house. The first they knew of the fire was by Mrs Hemmings waking up and smelling smoke. She immediately aroused her husband, who called the servant. The fire had by that time got well hold of the house, so that their attention had to be turned to the best means of escape. It was found impossible to descend the staircase, and the window was the only means by which they could leave the house. A ladder was procured by a man outside and placed against the wall, by which the occupants all descended.

Mr Tiltman, who lives in an apartment at the front of the building, ran into the High-street, half dressed, where he met police constable Bourne on duty, who promptly raised the alarm, aroused Mr John Laurence, the superintendent of the fire brigade. The keys of the fire engine house, which are kept at the George Hotel, having been obtained ... the engine (which is kept at the Town Hall, within a few yards of the scene of the fire) was soon got to work.

By the united energies of a large number of willing workers of all classes of society, the fire was happily confined to where it originated. His Worship the Mayor and other members of the Watch committee were most assiduous in offering suggestions and also assisted at the pumps. The fire engine might be seen at times manned by clergymen, tradesmen, shop-assistants, and labourers, all working with a hearty good will for one common object − the saving of property from destruction.

Happily a quantity of rain fell during the night and this perhaps helped to stay the progress of the flames; but certain it is that had not the utmost promptitude been used the most serious results would have followed. In about three hours after the first alarm the Red Lion, with that portion occupied by Mr Tiltman, was a heap of smoking ruins, and presented a scene of devastation seldom witnessed in so short a time; the houses being old, and a great deal of wood in them fed the flames, which raged and licked with fiery tongues the adjacent property with threatening attitude. As rafter after rafter fell with a terrible crash, the flames shot up high into the air and together with large sparks traversed a long distance. The sparks entered the open window of a house some distance off, which took fire but was soon quenched.

The property destroyed, which is worth a considerable sum of money, is insured in the Sun Fire Office, the furniture being insured in the Norwich Union. The Court Harold Order of Foresters held their meetings at the Lion, and the valuable banners, regalia, &c., were destroyed, the books, which were in the custody of the secretary, being the only articles saved.

The fireman continued to throw water on the smoking ruins during the day and all danger of a further outbreak appeared to be at an end.[8]

The Red Lion was never rebuilt but a new Board School opened on the site in 1874. At the opening ceremony the Reverend Frank Proctor, a temperance campaigner, made the following insulting remarks: 'The location of this school is due to an accident and probably one of the happiest events was that most useful fire which destroyed the Red Lion. I think, as long as the poor old red fellow wagged his tale, we would have hesitated in taking him down and destroying his old location (laughter).'

Thus, 300 years of the Red Lion and of Rye history was shamefully dismissed in a mean and despicable manner.[9]

Ship
Strand

After 1950

At one time the building now known as the Ship Inn was part of a complex of riverside warehouses used by the Excise for the storage of smuggler's contraband. Periodically the Excise would auction off accumulated contraband to the highest bidder, and naturally potential buyers wanted to taste the goods before buying. Over time an ad hoc bar was established to cater for this demand.

This bar was the forerunner of the Ship Inn and an early deed informs us that in 1722 it was known as the Cock and Coney (making the Ship around 300 years old).[1]

In his book: *Smuggling in Rye and District*, historian K M Clark explains that the Romney Marsh smugglers were so large and daring by the 1780s, and smuggling had grown to such an extent, that nothing short of a whole regiment of cavalry would have been sufficient to put it down. But because of the American War of Independence no troops were available. It is little wonder that Lord Pembroke in 1781 asked the question: "Will Washington take America, or the smugglers England first? The bet would be a fair even one."

This quotation along with the names of several local revenue cutters (customs boats), and men of war from the 18th and early 19th centuries, adorns the front wall of the Ship today.

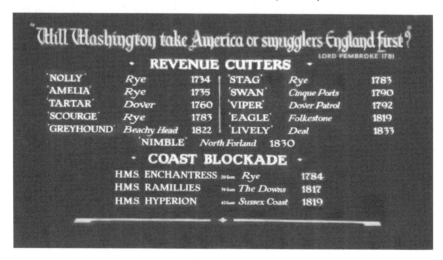

A century later in the 1820s the name Cock and Coney was changed to the Duke of Wellington, and then changed again to the Ship Inn around 1836 when it was fully licensed.[2]

The Ship was sold by Rye Corporation to St Leonards Brewery in 1853 and a valuation of the property in 1854 tells us that the Ship had six bedrooms (there are 10 today), and five public rooms— bar parlour, bar, tap room, a sitting room for guests staying overnight and a games room for billiards and bagatelle.[3] The games room was the location of the 'gambling' incident which took place in 1892 (see page 202).

Also on the ground floor there was a kitchen, store and wash house. The house contents without stock, were valued at £28.16s.

At the end someone had written in pencil: 'Deduct two weeks rent at £1. 4s.'[4]

A number of women ran the Ship in the 1860s without, it seems, much luck, or any comments from the magistrates about female licensees, which was unusual. In 1861 Eliza Flanaghan apparently had a tough time and lasted only a few months. The next licensee was cautioned in advance by the magistrates 'in respect of the notorious character the house had obtained'.

Three years later, in 1864, landlady Mary Prior, wife of Richard Prior, was a court witness to a charge against William Clarke, a beer house keeper in the Mint. Clarke was charged with using obscene language in the Strand by P C Wood. Landlady Mary Prior and other witnesses from among the Ship's customers, all spoke out against P C Wood 'who wanted to lock them all up', in a show of support for the beer house keeper. The case was dismissed but in a second case in the same year, Richard Prior denied that the Ship 'was a resort of bad characters and said there were several other houses which such characters used and they were not looked after', ie they went unchallenged by the police.

From the mid 19th century it was custom and practice for certain public houses to provide basic banking facilities for customers who didn't have a bank account. Among this class of customer were army pensioners who drew a pension every quarter. There are at least three examples in Rye of army pensioners using public houses for this purpose: in 1860 at the Cinque Ports Arms, in 1865 at the Red Lion Inn and in 1888 at the Ship. How the withdrawal process worked is not entirely clear but it seems that publicans had some sort of arrangement with the War Office. However, these transactions were not always orderly, straightforward affairs. The following example was reported in the local press in 1888:

AN ARMY RESERVE MAN

On Wednesday last a labourer of Sandhurst named David Couchman was charged with being drunk and refusing to quit the Ship Inn. A Police Constable said: "At about 2.30pm yesterday I was summonsed to the Ship Inn. Defendant was inside using bad language. The landlord asked defendant, who had taken his boots off, to go outside, and after considerable persuasion he left. He was unable to take care of himself and I took him to the lockup."

Joseph Bailey, landlord of the Ship Inn said the man entered his house about 2.30pm. "I refused to serve him with liquor and he became very abusive. The man said he was an Army Reserve man, and came to the Ship to take his money. He gave a man some of his money to take care of, but could not afterwards find him." The Mayor said he was very sorry when men came to Rye to take their pensions they did not behave in a better manner. Defendant would be fined 5s and 8s costs and the bench hoped he would not act so foolishly in the future. The money was paid.[5]

Another public house custom found at the Ship was that of 'scoring', the name given to an early form of credit provided by some landlords for beer served over the bar.

KEEPING A SCORE
A shipwright, called Leaf Dunk asked the advice of the court with regard to an act of the landlord of the Ship Inn, Charles Pippett. He said he went to the house for a quart of beer and proffered a sovereign, but Pippett kept back 6s for some drink he and a man named Cranford had some time ago, and which should not have been 'scored' to him. He refused to give him the money, and he (Dunk) asked their Worships what he could do to get it back. The Mayor advised him to go to a solicitor. It was more to do with the County Court than a Magisterial Bench.[6]

In the 1890s, to accommodate all these drinkers, the Ship tap room became a Four Ale Bar. This proved popular and was followed by the introduction of a more upmarket Six Ale Bar. Four Ale was simply the brewery's cheapest beer at four pence a quart [1d a pint] while Six Ale was a better quality ale at sixpence a quart. These two bars were the equivalent of the more common public bar and the bar parlour.[7]

However, not all was plain sailing. In 1892 the Ship experienced a threat to its very existence, when a simple application for the transfer of the licence from one landlord to another was refused, the magistrates declaring they would close the Ship down. Following this, the brewery appealed at the Quarter Sessions where eventually the Rye decision was overturned.

However, during the Lewes appeal some interesting facts emerged. One was that a previous landlord had been dismissed by

the brewery because he was convicted for allowing gambling on the premises. The 'gambling incident' was described by a witness as: "A set of rowdies, who are very well known in the neighbourhood, were in the habit of visiting all new landlords, and coming into the house for the purpose of taking the skin off the landlord's eyes." This was a local catch phrase for getting as much beer as possible for nothing.

'The landlord refused to serve them after which they created a disturbance, and the ringleader, a man called Jacobs, wanted to fight

Why not visit the new

GRANARY BAR

at the

SHIP INN

THE STRAND, RYE

Morning Coffee   —   Luncheons   —   Dinner

DINING ROOM AVAILABLE FOR FUNCTIONS

ACCOMMODATION

PHONE RYE 2233

the landlord. The police were called, the men were turned out and Jacobs was prosecuted.'

'At the hearing Jacobs called a witness, not to prove that he was innocent, but to prove that the landlord allowed gambling on the premises. The landlord admitted that he played, or someone played, a game of bagatelle for a glass of beer and he was convicted of allowing gambling. Consequently, he had to give up the licence.' Eventually, St Leonard's Brewery was allowed to install a new landlord and the Ship moved on.[8]

In 1913 St Leonard's Brewery and its seven tied houses were leased by Breeds Brewery of Hastings. Of the seven tied houses, the Ship, Rye and the Broad Oak, Brede, were the only St Leonards Brewery pubs outside of Hastings. Breeds purchased the freehold of the Ship in 1930 but was itself bought out by George Beer and Rigden of Faversham in 1931.

In 1933 Rye Town Council was busy reconstructing and widening Undercliff Road to create a new route around the town. A new road surface and pavement were raised in the reconstruction which allowed surface water to penetrate into the doorways and entrances of the Ship, causing damage to the pub and danger to customers. The brewers were awarded £100 compensation.[9]

A 1939 rate assessment showed the Ship had a private bar, a public bar, a smoke room, a living room, a sitting room and six bedrooms, suggesting that there had not been much structural

BREEDS & CO.,
Pale Ale & Stout Brewers,
THE HASTINGS BREWERY,

HASTINGS.

LIST OF PRICES OF BEER IN CASK.

		Per Barrel. 36 Galls.	Per Kil. 18 Galls.	Per Firkin. 9 Galls.	Per Pin. 4½ Galls.
LB	Light Bitter Beer	32/-	16/-	8/-	4/-
BB	Bitter Beer (Family Pale Ale) ... ` ...	36/-	18/-	9/-	4/6
BA	Bitter Ale	42/-	21/-	10/6	5/3
PA	Pale Ale	48/-	24/-	12/-	6/-
IPA	India Pale Ale	54/-	27/-	13/6	6/9
No. 1	Mild Ale	36/-	18/-	9/-	4/6
,, 2	,, ,, ...	54/-	27/-	13/6	6/9
P	Porter	36/-	18/-	9/-	4/6
S	Stout	42/-	21/-	10/6	5/3
SS	Double Stout	54/-	27/-	13/6	6/9
SSS	Extra Double Stout	62/-	31/-	...	..

LIST OF PRICES OF BEER IN BOTTLE.

		Imperial Pints.				Imperial Pints.
Bitter Beer	... ...	per doz. 2/3	Cooper	... ...	per doz. 2/6
Pale Ale ...	... ...	,, 2/6	Single Stout	... ...	,, 2/6
India Pale Ale ...	... ...	,, 3/-	Double ,,	... ...	,, 3/-

HOPS.—It is guaranteed that no substitutes for Hops are used at the Hastings Brewery.

All Beers delivered Carriage Paid to any Station on the L. B. & S. C. Ry. and S. E. Ry.

TELEGRAPHIC ADDRESS: "BREEDS, HASTINGS."

1890

change since 1854 although the 'Four Ale' and 'Six Ale' bars had long gone. Draymen delivered three times a week and expected a pint each. Charabanc drivers also expected cigarettes or a drink or took their charabancs elsewhere.

Three years later the Ship was damaged in a German air raid. Some men working on the roof of the already damaged pub were killed in a second raid. The Ship however, remained intact.

Ship Inn today

Standard Inn and the Swan
Mint

1938–1940

These two public houses on the Mint were next door neighbours for 43 years. Both arrived late on the scene in the 1860s, to join a third public house – the long established Foresters Arms – two doors away.

The magistrates noted the proximity of these three pubs, but concluded that they as magistrates would have more control over them as fully licensed premises than they would as beer houses only answerable to the Excise.

The Standard and the Swan were located in premises dating from the 15th century and both were probably licensed premises centuries before. A recent building survey has suggested that the Standard's medieval design initially included a ground floor beer shop or tap room, accessible directly from the street. The Swan probably had a similar design and if this is subsequently found to be the case it could put both pubs on an equal historical footing with the Mermaid.

Soon after its first licence was granted around 1860, the Swan 'and the property next door', possibly the Standard, were put up for sale by the assignees of the estate of Jeremiah Smith. Thus both properties possibly belonged to him during the 'treating scandal' and his imprisonment seven years before.

The Swan had a reputation for being one of the quietest pubs in Rye. As someone remarked: "The Swan wasn't happy as a pub and was always regarded as the Standard's little sister, the pub next door."

As far as is known there was never any incident in the Swan involving customers or landlords, with the exception of one drunken sailor in 1879.

Jack Barber, a sailor from Hastings, was charged by the Rye Borough Bench with being drunk and disorderly at the Swan, Mint. A Police Constable said: "About eleven o'clock on Monday evening I was in the Mint and saw defendant come out of the Swan. He was drunk and using offensive language. He pulled off his coat and wanted to fight some of the people in the public house. 'I'll fight the lot of 'em if they come out here one at a time.' Two or three men then noticed that I was standing near, and took hold of defendant and led him away. I had seen the defendant drunk in the street the

c1910

previous evening, and then had reason to caution him." He was fined
1s [5p]with 9s [45p] costs or 10 days imprisonment with hard labour.[1]

In the 1870s and later, the Rye Licensed Victuallers Association
drew up a campaign to sell tea, in opposition to local grocers who
sold beer and spirits. The LVA policy was 'to consider the advisability
of Licensed Victuallers near to any grocer who retails anything in
our line of business, undertaking to sell tea and all tinned goods,
such as coffee, salmon, lobster and milk at cost price, until such
grocers consent to give up their licences'.

"Licensed grocers", they said, "were doing all they could to take
the bread out of the mouths of licensed victuallers and their wives
and families". Several Rye publicans joined the campaign including

Alfred Jarrett of the Standard, who had the policy announced by the Town Crier![2] This was seen facetiously as:-

A BLESSING

The Licensed Victuallers of Rye considering that the grocers had intruded upon their province by selling wine and spirits, have taken in revenge to selling tea. On Thursday last Mr Alfred Jarrett announced through the town crier that he could supply good tea at 2s 6d a pound. Other publicans are following in his footsteps. This is a capital arrangement especially for old ladies troubled with 'sinkings' and rather given to taking divers 'drops o'somethin' short'. Calumny must die. Who enters a public house in future goes for tea and not for gin.[3]

London tea suppliers advertised in Rye:

The Licensed Victuallers' Pure Tea Company's Agents,
(Licensed Victuallers only) supply

TEAS   CHOICE,   PURE,   AND UNADULTERATED,
At the lowest possible prices.

BLACK.—First crop Black Tea, packed in orange wrappers, at 2s 6d per lb.
MIXED.— Finest Mixed Tea, packed in chocolate wrappers, at 3s. 6d per lb.
GREEN.— Finest Moynne Green Tea, in light-green wrappers, at 3s. 6d per lb.
INDIAN. —Assam Indian very fine Black Tea, in dark blue and gold wrappers, at 3s. 6d per lb.
In packets of ½., ¼., and 2oz., and in canisters of 2lbs., 4lbs., and 8lbs.

Each packet bears trade mark, name and price.
Be careful to obtain the Pure Tea Company's Teas.
Wholesale depot: George F. Smyth, Manager.
DENMAN STREET, LONDON BRIDGE, S.E.
Carriage paid on parcels of 30lbs, and upwards.

1873

When a new Licensing Act became law in 1904 the magistrates invited local brewers to nominate pubs for closure. Most publicans were naturally opposed to the idea and the Licensed Victualler's Association advised their members not to participate.

The Swan was the only pub in Rye to go against the stream. Brewers Edwin Finn of Lydd applied for an addition to the licence of their stores in the Wish, to sell bottled beer in quantities of not less than a dozen pints. Edward Brown, landlord of the Swan, announced he was willing to give up his licence without compensation in exchange for the licence of the bottle store. This was agreed, the Swan closed down, and Brown then became the store manager. The Swan however, was the only Rye pub to be voluntarily surrendered for closure under the 1904 Licensing Act. This was seen at the time as quite controversial, and the Finn Brewery fell out of favour for a while.[4]

After its closure in 1906 the premises became the 'Old Swan Fishmongers', run by George Jarrett who formerly owned the herring deeze behind the Pipemaker's Arms. The closure of the Foresters and the Swan gave an obvious boost to the trade of the Standard, which then became pro-active with a football team, slate club, Town Band nights and 'Smokers'.

EDWIN FINN & SONS, Ltd., ❁

❁ Pale Ale Brewers,

BOTTLED BEER MERCHANTS,

AERATED WATER MANUFACTURERS

(These Waters have been passed through a Pasteur (Chamberland) Filter, therefore, are Absolutely Pure)

LYDD, KENT.

Agent for Rye and District—E. F. BROWN.

Office and Stores—WISH STREET, RYE.

A typical 'convivial gathering' of the Slate Club was reported when 40 members sat down to an excellent spread, songs, music and drinking each other's health. £26 was paid out to sick members that year and the 'share-out' was £1. 2s 7d [£1.13p] for each of 140 members. The chairman noted however, that a new slate club had been started in the town 'by a number of religious bodies' (ie temperance organisations), 'and would perhaps take away some members by offering bigger things'.

In 1907, two football teams, the Standards and the New Inners, played a charity match on the Salts. The following is an edited report of the game.

AMUSING EXHIBITION OF 'FOOTBALL' BY SLATE CLUB MEMBERS

With the object of assisting the Rye Borough Nursing Fund, a 'football' match was arranged on Tuesday afternoon on the Town Salts, between teams representing the 'New Inn' and 'Standard' Slate Clubs. The event was favoured with sunny weather, and there was a very large number of spectators on the ground.

The teams, on forming up, presented a somewhat picturesque sight, each player having donned the coloured shirt that best suited his fancy. Four or five of the competitors however, played to much advantage in garbs characteristic of the 'tan frock' brotherhood. In passing, it might also be mentioned that a good percentage of the contestants had passed the matured age of 40.

The kicking-off ceremony was performed by Councillor H J Gasson, JP, and there spontaneously followed a mighty stampede for the sphere. The backs and half-backs at times ably led the way, and it was then noticed that New Inn showed a slight superiority over their opponents, some of whom had affixed on their shirts the blazoned standard of their side. Corners were plentiful, and the subsequent melee in front of the goal inevitably resulted in the veteran players frantically falling prostrate in their ecstasy on to the ground. For a considerable time before the half-time the sphere was kept in midfield, neither team being able to break through the other's stalwart defence. The forwards kicked the ball about with great gusto, and the backs showed no lack of intelligence in the use of hands, but referee Cooper, whose decisions were somewhat original, paid no heed to such insignificant incidents, and magnanimously allowed play to proceed.

The second half saw great activity on the part of both teams. It was evident that scoring somehow would result, and this happened about ten minutes after the restart through Bridger (1–0). The New Inners became more than ever desperately earnest in their endeavour to equalise, but their eagerness was to be punished, and the Standards came again, and after a prolonged scrimmage, lustily bombarded their enemies goal. The backs and half-backs fisted out with commendable vigour, and the goalie worked as hard and deservingly cleared.

But the Standards were not to be denied, and it was due to Dunk that their lead was further increased (2–0) with a remarkably fine shot. An extraordinary run on the part of New Inn ensued, and from this Bennett came out triumphant (2–1). Things now looked very hot, and more especially with the animated beings in the costumes of the fishing fraternity, and it was evident that the Standard was still desirous of adding a third one. Their expectation was realised through the enterprise of Bridger (3–1). A general play of hands ensued, but nothing happened until a few minutes before time, when Bennett found the net for New Inn (3–2).

During the progress of the game, which proved amusing, though at times the interest seemed to relax, several members of the fair sex were busy collecting on behalf of the fund.
1907

A smoking concert was held at the Standard Inn that evening, when the money that had been collected was counted. The proceedings were interspersed with songs, before it was announced that the collection amounted to £4. 6s. Mrs Bray collected the highest amount (£1. 5s 10d) and was presented by Mr Halliwell with a gold brooch. Mr Bray, who received the gift on behalf of his wife, suitably returned thanks. A 'whip round' resulted in the sum collected being increased to £5. 1s (a record collection). It was decided that £5 should be given to the Nursing Fund.

In February 1913 the Standard was the chosen venue for an annual reunion of the Rye Town Band. In a short speech the bandleader described the band as 'all working class', and said its aim was 'to provide popular music for the Rye public to enliven the dull moments'. The band then accompanied the Iden Sextet who entertained 'the assembled customers with some admirably rendered songs'.

In the inter-war period and during the Second World War the Standard was the venue for at least four clubs: a Buffaloes Lodge, a Slate Club, a Birthday Club and the Social Brothers Benefit Society.

Standard Inn and Swan Cottage Tea Rooms today

Tower

Landgate

1866–1870

The Tower Inn, Landgate was a late arrival on the Rye pub scene. It was not listed in the local street directory until 1845 and seems to have opened in about 1840.

From the beginning the Tower led a quiet life, and nothing much was heard of this pub in the early years. It has only one conviction on record, that in 1862 when landlord Robert Dunk was fined 5s [25p] for allowing people on the premises 'during the hours of divine service', after a police constable found two men hiding in the back yard.

Between 1866 and 1874 the landlord was William Mills, whose custom was drawn mainly from the Rye shipyards of G & T Smith and Hoad Brothers Ltd.

Shipyard workers

Luckily for his customers Mills had a social conscience and in 1866 decided to campaign against their long hours of work. The campaign, dubbed the Four O'Clock Movement, was followed in the local press:-

SATURDAY AFTERNOON FOUR O'CLOCK MOVEMENT
On Friday evening last, a large and influential meeting of mechanics (principally shipwrights), was held in the Working Men's Institution, to receive the report of the delegates on the above subject. Mr William Mills, of Landgate, presided. After some conversation, in which it was averred that it was a general cause

for the well being of all, and therefore whatever was done, should be done in a spirit of unity, without division or unpleasant feelings towards anyone, Mr John Moon was called upon to state the result of the interview between the delegates and their employers. Mr Moon replied that they waited upon Messrs. Hoad at six o'clock that evening, and told them that the boon they sought was to be allowed to leave off work at four o'clock on Saturday afternoons, a practice now adopted in most large firms throughout the kingdom. Messrs. Hoad thought this request was somewhat unreasonable, but ultimately expressed their willingness to meet the wishes of the men by allowing them to leave work at half-past four on Saturday afternoons, and that if this proposition were acceded to, the bell should be rung at that time to-morrow. They expressed a wish that the men should keep punctual time in future, but with respect to ringing the bell at six o'clock in the morning – as had been suggested – they did not wish it. A man might occasionally oversleep himself, and they had no wish to be too hard, but each party should endeavour to consider each other's interest. In reply to a question, Mr Moon said that everything else was to go on as usual, so that if a man did not go to work till nine on Saturday morning he would be paid for three-quarters of a day as heretofore. Another conversation ensued, which ended in a proposition, duly seconded, that the masters' offer be accepted. An amendment was ultimately moved and seconded in favour of four o'clock. On a show of hands the original proposition was carried. – The Chairman said it was a well-known fact that he was a strong supporter of the four o'clock movement, because he considered it was just. Votes of thanks were most heartily accorded to the Chairman for the deep interest he had taken in the matter, warmly applauding his straightforward reply to an anonymous letter, and assuring him they reposed the greatest confidence in his disinterested integrity; and to the delegates for the trouble they had taken in bringing the matter to an issue. A collection was made in the room, 5s contributed for the institution, as an acknowledgment for the use of the room, and the party dispersed. – On Saturday afternoon all the shipwrights and most other mechanics quitted their employment for the week at half-past four, and appeared much pleased with the concession thus far made to their request.[1]

Not everyone in the town welcomed the above decision which elicited some anonymous correspondence. Mills replied accordingly:-

THE SHIPWRIGHTS AND THEIR EMPLOYERS
To the Editor, of the South Eastern Advertiser

Sir, – In a paper professing itself the advocate of the rights of the toiling classes, there appeared on March 17th a letter signed 'A Shipwright'. In that a statement was made respecting his class of workmen and how they were worked, and the number of hours they were obliged to toil. Will you allow me to give the public further information on the subject?

The shipwrights of Rye work from daylight until dark in the winter – the same as in other ports – and for the last six weeks they have worked four and a half hours per week more than other shipwrights. Men employed in other ports – with one exception, I believe, namely, Sandwich – never work after half-past five at any time of the year, excepting when they make overtime. From the 25th of March to the 29th of September, it is customary in Rye to allow the shipwrights half an hour for tea. Through the six summer months, the men work one hour and a half per week more on Saturday than men employed at other ports; and for about six weeks after the 29th of September they work four hours and a half per week more than shipwrights at other places. As regards over time, men in Rye work ten hours a day, but in other ports only eight hours are required for a day.

I leave your readers to judge for themselves if the mechanics of Rye have asked of their employers an unreasonable favour. It is now turned twenty years since the four o'clock movement was first originated. One town in Sussex had that favour granted them twenty years ago. It appears that all men in seaport towns have obtained the privilege of leaving work at 4 o'clock on Saturdays, and I think, Mr. Editor, now that the Saturday early closing movement has travelled all round Great Britain, it ought to be expected that Rye will at last receive justice though it should come twenty years behind. As to the other remark of the 'Shipwright', of inducing men to spend money and time in a public house, I trust they have more command over themselves.

If the writer calling himself 'A Shipwright' had been present at our meetings in the Union Rooms, he would probably not have been so prompt in his condemnation of our proceedings.

I remain, dear Sir
Yours obediently

Chairman of the 4 o'clock movement.
Landlord of a little public house in Landgate²

STEAM
Communication
<small>WITH</small>
BOULOGNE.

THAT FAST, COMMODIOUS SEA-GOING VESSEL.

The WINDSOR CASTLE, John Murray, Commander,
The EDINBURGH CASTLE, W.Barry. Commander,
WILL

Leave RYE for BOULOGNE
On SATURDAY, THE 25TH INST.
AT 8 O'CLOCK IN THE MORNING,
And continue running, according to the time of Tide, every

WEDNESDAY & SATURDAY,
Returning the following THURSDAY and MONDAY,
UNTIL FURTHER NOTICE.

FARES: TO BOULOGNE, 7S.6d. AND 5s; FROM BOULOGNE, 5s,
CARRIAGES, 2 Guineas.   HORSES, 1 Guinea.

These splendid Vessels, unequalled on the Coast for Accommodation, have
lately undergone most extensive Repairs in their Engines: rendering them, in
every respect, a very desirable medium of Communication.
The greatest punctuality will be observed in starting, and every regulation
used to ensure comfort and safety to the Passengers.

Messrs. ALLEN & FOWLE, Rye, AGENTS,
UNDER THE SUPERINTENDENCE OF A COMMITTEE.

Another landlord in another year, Thomas Dale in the 1880s, organised steamer trips to Boulogne with the Tower Outing Club. This club was a target of the temperance campaigners because the trips were run on Sundays, the only day most of his customers could go, and because the steamer company had a bar on board. The temperance lobby thought all drink should be prohibited on Sundays and all pubs and bars closed on that day.

They were also opposed to the sale of alcoholic drinks which were claimed to be healthy, or had medicinal properties or which were advertised as 'good for you'. Such drinks included local brews such as Rye Milk Punch and Romney Marsh Sloe Gin 'for the winter', brewed by Chapman's and sold in the Tower and elsewhere; Mackeson's Milk Stout brewed at Hythe and believed to be anti-rheumatic and to be 'recommended by the medical profession'. Another drink was 'the finest rum: liquid sunshine'.

c1900

In 1910 the magistrate at the Brewster Sessions said: "We are not inclined to take any very drastic action. There are however, two licences which we consider should be referred for closure. One is the Jolly Sailor, respecting which complaints have been made and the other is the Tower, Landgate, which we deem unnecessary."

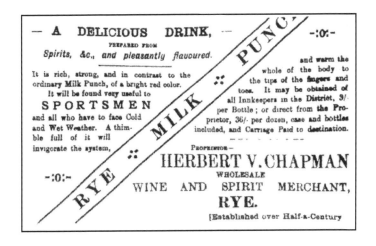

They noted that the Tower was a few doors from the Queen's Head with its assembly room and stables, and the Bedford Arms although close by was 'resorted to by people resident on Romney Marsh, Rye Harbour etc'.

But they admitted 'nothing could be alleged against the manner which Mr Taylor had conducted the business'. Thus unfairly, the Tower came to the end of its life.[3]

Tower today

Union Inn
East Street

1960s

The Union Inn was originally two 16th century cottages and a small shop. The cottages may have been licensed premises centuries ago, but by the 19th century the building was owned by John Swain and occupied by his under tenant John Hunter, who converted one of the cottages into the Union beer house in 1830.[1]

John Hunter was keen to become fully licensed, and applied annually over the next three years. His application was granted in 1833 when he became 'a fully licensed man'.

However, a full licence did not guarantee immediate success, and for some years he was self-employed as a tailor during the day while his wife Sarah ran the pub. John Hunter died in 1839, after which the licence was transferred to his widow.

In 1841 the pub was sold, and a deed tells us that: 'John Hunter, landlord and under tenant of John Swain, sometime since converted these premises into a public house bearing the sign of the Union Inn'.[2]

A valuation of the property in 1861 shows the licence was then held by their son James and thus, for 30 years the pub was run by the Hunter family. The valuation describes the Union at that time as a very small house, with only one public room separated into a bar and a bar parlour by a partition.

The valuation lists one bedroom with no accommodation for letting. It had a kitchen and wash house at the rear of the building and was attached to a small shop next door, possibly previously used by John Hunter as a tailoring shop. At some later date the pub was enlarged when the two cottages and the shop were integrated.

The valuation tells us that the bar parlour had seats fixed to the floor, shelving behind the bar and a zinc blind on two brass rods. Among the bar equipment was a 'spirit fountain', some ceramic spirit barrels with taps and fittings, a beer engine, another zinc blind on two brass rods and four stout metal bars supporting the partition.

Beer was only pulled in the bar, and parlour customers were served through a serving hatch in the partition. All tables and seats were fixed to the walls or the floor, and the bedroom was furnished with plain deal furniture.

The shop was basic with only a counter and shelving listed. The valuation points out, with some pride, that the pub sign was made of wrought iron, and was the first class work of a local blacksmith.[3]

The Union never appeared to have had a tap room, suggesting perhaps that the landlord was trying to move away from the beer house image, and seeking custom further up the social scale.

In the same year, 1861, the next landlord John Paine Munn was charged with having the pub open for the sale of beer at 1.30am on a Sunday morning and for refusing to admit the police. When a constable was finally admitted at ten minutes to two he found two drunks in the bar. Munn claimed they were lodgers and, as the law

𝕾𝖀𝕾𝕾𝕰𝕏 to wit.

WRIT OF INQUIRY.

Taylor, Printer, Rye.

WILLIAM the FOURTH, King, Defender of the Faith, and of his liege subjects' claim to his especial protection, as Guardian of their Health; To *his trusty Bailiffs, John Doe and Richard Roe, and his well-beloved Stewards of his Household, John Barleycorn and Harry Hop— Greeting: We command you, and every one of you, to summon every man in your Bailiwick to attend a Court, to be holden from* DAY TO DAY, *until further notice,* **at** *the Bar of our well-beloved subject,* **JOHN HUNTER, Union Inn, Rye,** *to examine and give judgment, according to the Statute made and provided, on his pure and unadulterated Malt Liquors, Spirits, &c., which he is selling at the following low Prices:*

Strong Cordial Gin, 4 1/2 d. per quartern; Cream of the Valley, 5d. ditto; Old Tom, 6d. ditto:; Rum, 6d. ditto; Cognac Brandy, 1s. ditto; Strong Sparkling Ale, 7d. per pot; Double Stout, 7 d. ditto; Good Beer, 3 1/2d. ditto.

Union Inn advertisement c1835

then stood, lodgers could be served at anytime. However, as the pub had only one bedroom we can assume they were not genuine lodgers.

In 1864 landlord Henry Baldwin suddenly gave up the licence, and it was felt that the Union might close if a new licensee was not quickly found.

Without a landlord the pub closed for a few months but attracted the attention of two of the town's more prominent licensees, who between them carried some status. These were George Austin, landlord of the Cinque Ports Arms and Henry Huckstepp, landlord of the George Tap.

George Austin first stepped in around September and took over the Union licence for a few months 'to ensure the continuity of this public house', ie to ensure it stayed open. This was one of few instances in Rye when the magistrates allowed an individual to hold more than one licence concurrently. Why the brewery did not act is unknown, but the Union may have been a 'Free House'. Austin was followed in December 1864 by Henry Huckstepp, who gave up the licence of the George Tap to run the Union which he saw as a small step up the social scale.[4]

By the late 1860s the Union was popular with local fishermen and boat owners. This patronage was reflected in the fact that a number of Coroner's Inquests into accidents and deaths in the fishing industry, were held here. The local bench also felt that fishermen who might be required to attend and participate in these inquests would be more comfortable in the Union than in the more formal surroundings of say, the Red Lion or the George.

Nevertheless, members of inquests were often required to inspect the body which was laid out in the pub. It was the local custom for members of Coroner's Inquests to adjourn to another pub after such a gruelling and harrowing experience. In the case of the Union, jurors usually went to the George Tap.

A typical inquest into the drowning of a fisherman in Rye Harbour, in 1881, was held in the Union Inn in May of that year, but failed to come to any conclusion as to how the 'accident' had happened. They could only agree that the deceased was 'found drowned in Rye Harbour'.[5]

The Union has also been associated with smuggling. At one time a building around the corner in Market Street had a pulley wheel installed in its chimney, which was used to haul kegs of brandy up into the attic. This contraband, so the legend goes, was then transferred through adjoining attics to finally reach the attic of the Union Inn! But as we shall see it was not only contraband moving between the attics.

In the 1930s the Union became a 'Goth pub' when it was acquired by the People's Refreshment House Association Ltd,[6] a temperance organisation influenced by the 'Gothenburg Model' of 'disinterested management'. The manager of the Union was described as an 'agent in the cause of temperance and good behaviour', was paid a fixed salary plus any profit from food and non-alcoholic drinks. All profits from alcohol were donated to local 'objects of public utility'. A few 'Goth pubs' still exist in Scotland. As far as is known the Union was the only one in Rye.

In later years the Union was a contender for most haunted pub in Rye. One ghost who resided there was apparently that of a young unmarried mother who died after being pushed down the cellar

Peoples Refreshment House Association sign

Explaining the principles of the Peoples Refreshment House Association 1907

steps in the 1850s. In 1993 researchers into spiritual phenomena witnessed banging and laser flashes, and the kitchen door opening and closing by itself.

Further investigations revealed that the landlord's young son had been visited by 'Postman Pat' at night, and that several other people staying overnight had experienced the ghost of a seaman in a blue jacket sometimes wearing a sou'wester. The old lady next door also experienced the seaman in her attic. We can only ask: Was this the ghost of an old smuggler moving contraband between the attics, or perhaps of the fisherman who drowned in the harbour in 1881?

Downstairs, the ghost of Emily, a young woman in a red dress, was often seen walking through the bar towards the cellar steps. She apparently died from a broken neck after being pushed down the cellar steps when pregnant. According to the Ghost Club investigators, Emily and her family lived in the middle cottage in 1856, and her father, a local mortician, was apparently ashamed of her pregnancy. However, when the investigators made contact with the ghost of Emily in 1992, she denied the baby was hers. The baby's remains were allegedly contained behind a glass brick in the rear dining room.

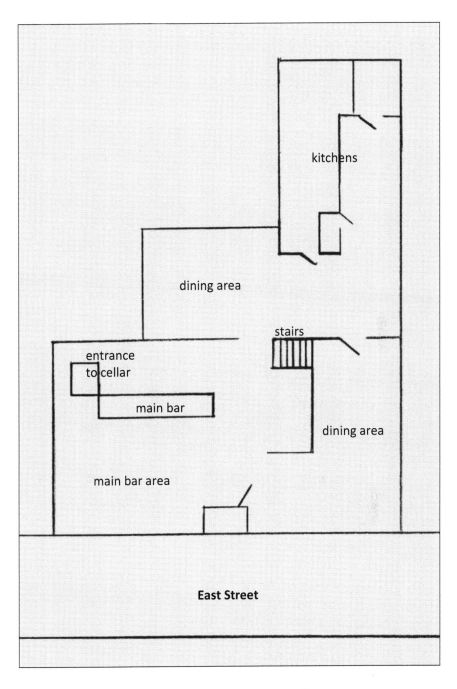

kitchens

dining area

stairs

entrance
to cellar

main bar

main bar area

dining area

East Street

Union Inn ground plan 1993 [7]

The pub was reputably rid of its ghosts in 1993 when exorcists rebalanced the pubs hidden ley-lines with a row of nine crystals.[8]

The Union was listed Grade 2 in 1951, including the projecting shop window with small square panes at the north corner, dating from the early 19th century.

Union Inn today

Ypres Castle Inn
Gun Garden

Ypres Castle Inn showing the original shop front, 1900s

The Ypres Castle Inn is named after the Ypres Castle, a tower of the same name at the top of Gun Garden steps. The castle itself is one of the oldest buildings in Rye, and dates from 1249 when it was built as part of a defence against constant raids by the French. The inn (known as 'Wipers' by today's customers), is mentioned as a licensed premises around 1833, but was probably licensed before that date.

An early landlord, George French, is listed in *Robson's Street Directory* for 1838 as a 'Beer Retailer, Gun Garden Steps', where he ran a pub, shop and off licence.

In 1863 when the licence was transferred from William Bourne to John Hyder, a valuation of the 'furniture and effects' was made by a local agent. At that time the pub consisted of the usual parlour and tap room but it also had a third bar known as a 'bar-shop'. The bar-shop, the former shop used by George French, was well stocked with spirits and a 'three-pull' beer engine, but was also equipped with three sets of copper scales and a number of copper weights for weighing fish.

Thus the bar-shop acted for a time as a 'retail fishmongers'. The magistrates appeared to agree with this as long as the shop didn't open for trade 'during the hours of divine service', ie on Sundays. Besides the tap room, shop, and parlour, the Ypres Castle Inn also had a sitting room, kitchen, servant's room, three bedrooms, wash house and a cellar.[1]

According to *Adams Guide to Rye*, this cellar was used for storing smuggler's contraband in the 18th century. In the 1780s the building was a 'well known rallying place of the "freebooters". Under the wooden floor of the entrance room was a huge vault, and cunningly devised apertures existed in the walls and ceilings, there being no dearth of storage room for contraband.'[2]

We are informed by local legend and the *Sussex Weekly Advertiser* that in the 1780s 'prohibited goods' were imported into Rye by a cutter called the 'Good Intent' and deposited in this cellar. However, in 1788 the 'Good Intent' was seized by customs but retaken by the smugglers. It was reported that the cutter 'was carried away by divers persons unknown, who after fastening down in the cabin, John Amon, an extra Tidewaiter who had care of the said vessel, stood out to sea about two miles, and then put him in a boat and rowed him ashore about half a mile westward of the new harbour of Rye.' The 'Good Intent' then took off for France. The customs offered a £100 reward for the capture of the offenders.

DESCRIPTION of the Perfons, who rowed
the OFFICER on Shore.

The one a tall Man, near fix Feet high, of a dark Complexion, wore his own dark Hair falling on his Shoulders, had on a round Hat, and was dreffed in a fhort, dark-coloured Sailor's Jacket, and appeared to be about 30 Years of Age.

The other a fhorter and much ftouter Man, of a light Complexion, had a white Woollen cap on his Head over his Hair, which appeared to be light-brown colour, was dreffed in a fhort dark-coloured Sailor's Jacket and long Trowfer, and appeared to be about 40 or 50 Years of Age.

CUSTOM-HOUSE, RYE, 1ft of February, 1788.

T.P.LAMB, Collector.

R.BUTLER, Dep.Comp.

The 1863 valuation also listed a variety of traditional Victorian pub games and equipment. Included in the list were the usual indoor games of cards, dominoes, draughts and cribbage but also the outdoor games of quoits and bat and trap which were played in the pub garden. Both games are now virtually extinct.

Quoits is a traditional game which involves the throwing of metal rings over a set distance, to land over or near a spike called a hob, mott, or pin. It was extensively played by Rye fishermen in the garden of the Ypres Castle Inn, at the Queens Head, on the Crown Field, and outside the Queen Adelaide.

On the other hand the game of bat and trap at the Ypres Castle Inn is only one of two examples of the game being played in Rye that has come to light. It was played between two teams of up to eight players — one team batting and the other bowling. The game involves placing a heavy rubber ball on one end of a 'trap', which is a low wooden box 22 inches [560 mm] long, 5 inches wide [560mm] and 5 inches high, on top of which is a simple see-saw mechanism. Each batter in turn hits the opposite end of the lever (the 'striker') with a bat, so as to propel the ball into the air, and then attempts to hit the ball between two high posts situated 21 yards (19m) away and 13 feet 6 inches (4.11m) apart, at the other end of the pitch.

The trap and wicket

The bowling side stand behind and between the posts attempting to catch the ball before it hits the ground. The batsman is out if the ball is caught or if he or she fails to hit the ball between the posts at a height not exceeding 7 feet (2.1m). After each successful hit, a fielder aims the ball at the 'wicket' which is a 5-inch (130mm) square target at the end of the trap. If the bowler hits the wicket the batsman is 'bowled out'. If the bowler does not succeed, the batsman scores one run and continues to play. Once all the members of the first batting team have played, the batting and bowling teams change places.[3]

In the early 1900s the Ypres Castle Slate Club was active organising smoking concerts for charity in support of Hastings Hospital. On one occasion it was reported that 'there was a good attendance though most of the fishermen were out in their boats as the evening was favourable'. The majority of the active members of the slate club were also members of the Rye Borough Bonfire Boys, which used the Ypres Castle Inn as its headquarters in the years before the First World War.[4]

The original Ypres Castle sign was designed and painted by Kathleen Claxton at Wateringbury, Kent in 1939. After the Second World War Whitbread's Brewery, to which the Ypres Castle was then tied, issued miniature pub signs for a large number of their pubs in the south-east. These miniatures were given out with pints of beer and collected like cigarette cards or match-box labels. At first they were printed on thin aluminium sheet because of the post war paper

Ypres Castle c1939

shortage. Only later were they printed on thin card. There were two miniatures issued for public houses in Rye; the Queen Adelaide and the Ypres Castle Inn. Today these cards are considered valued collector's items and are traded on the internet.

Located in a pretty and picturesque position overlooking the River Rother and Rye harbour, and clad in traditional Sussex weather boarding, the Ypres Castle Inn has been much photographed. Possibly the most famous photograph, or at least most well known, was that taken by Eric De Mare in 1993 for the English Heritage National Monuments Record set up in the 1970s.

Ypres Castle Inn today

APPENDIX 1
Register of Licensees for Rye

Albion Commercial Inn, Rope Walk (Cinque Ports Street)

1839	William Aylward, (**Albion Brewery)**
1858	James Hobbs Starr
1859	James Gasson
1860	James Nye
1860	(closed)

Barley Mow BH, Landgate

1832–1845	George Dann

Bedford Arms, Fishmarket Road

1835–1848	William Apps
1848–1856	George Dann
1859–1887	William Relf
1887–1907	Charles Crowhurst
1907–1922	John Marsh
1927–1938	Charles Olley
1940–1941	Leslie Blackman
1941–1946	Daisy Blackman
1946	Leslie Blackman

Borough Arms, Strand

1592	John Hammond (**Blew Anchor**)
1728–1733	Joseph Tucker (**London Trader**)
1735	Robert Poire
1739–1776	Thomas Marley
1777–1782	John Swain
1782	Thomas Bourne
1783–1785	James King
1786	James Honiss
1787–1788	Edward Honiss
1789–1792	Mary Honiss (widow)
1792–1798	Michael Tiltman
1799	Thomas Pilcher

1800	William Watson
1801–1811	Michael Tiltman
1811–1830	James Crowhurst
1830–1834	Ann Crowhurst
1838–1840	James Shearer
1845	Judith Sargent
1852–1853	George Austin
1858	John Christmas
1859–1868	James Crowhurst
1868	Ann Crowhurst
1895	**(Borough Arms)**
1878–1901	John Shunn
1901	George Parkes Wood (brewery agent)
1901	Thomas Buckland
1901	Walter Hills
1902–1903	John Campbell
1903	George King
1903	Edward Law
1906	(closed)

Bull(s) Head, High Street

1634	
1702	Samuel Stretton
1715	John Coleman
1724	John Welch
1735	Richard Dawes
	John Waters
1737–1739	Francis Jewhurst
	William Payne
1752–1756	Thomas Hovenden
1756	(closed)

Chequer, The Butchery

Cinque Ports Arms, Cinque Ports Street

1820	
1824–1838	Thomas Lancaster
1838	Thomas Archer
1839	Jane Gorham
1846–1853	Charles Paul
1858–1865	George Austin
1870–1884	Mercer Hatch

1884–1887	Mrs E Hatch
1890–1899	Alfred Vidler jnr
1900–1905	John Reader
1905–1908	Harry Mountain
1908	Harold Finn
1908–1922	Alfred Clark
1922	James W Woodcock
1925	E Elliot
1930	Walter Barber
1933–1938	Frank Hollebon
1938–1940	A E Farley
1940–1942	Audrey Wright & William Burnham
1942	bombed and closed
1942–1946	Audrey Wright & Willliam Burnham (held licence 'in suspension' for the brewery)

Cinque Ports / Railway, Cinque Ports Street

1838–1839	Edgar Brignald (**Horse & Groom**)
1845–1853	William Richardson
1858–1859	George Allaway
1862–1868	Ben Heaver
1868–1869	William Norman (**Horse & Groom, Railway Commercial Inn**)
1870	William Verrall
1874–1890	Robert Jones
1891–1894	Albert Martin (**Railway Inn**)
1894–1896	Charles Gurr
1898–1899	J Reader
1899–1907	Edward Banister
1907–1908	William Ballard
1909–1910	James Dann
1910	Thomas Foster
1910–1912	Arthur Camp
1913–1918	James Elsemere
1925–1933	A J Clarke
1938	D H Mill
1939–1941	Frederick Foord
1941–1946	Gwendoline Muriel Marsden
1968	John McGrath (**Cinque Ports**)

Clarke's BH, The Mint

| 1864 | William Clarke |

Crown, Ferry Road

1839	Edward Barnes (**Crown &Sceptre**)
1858	Frederick King
1859–1899	Isaac Wright (**Crown Railway Inn**)
1899	William Wright
1900	Edward Cheeseman (**Crown**?)
1902–1903	Horace Tucker
1903	James Lewis
1907	Samuel Coleman
1907–1909	James Pilgrim
1909	Hartley Cross
1909–1915	Edward Roffey
1915	Walter Buckman
1915–1922	Edward Roffey
1927	Valentine Francis
1930	Weatherly Phipson
1932	Harold Tompkins
1938–1943	Albert Pawsey

Crowne, West Street

1520	John Sutton
1562	

Dial, 101 High Street

1830s	Thomas Earl (**Black Boy and Still**)
	William Payne
	Sarah Barnes
	Charles Pilcher
	Edward Hilder
	Thomas Bourne (**Dial**) ?
	Henry Bourne
1854–1875	Stephen Fryman ?
1878	Egbert Fryman
1878	(closed)

Dolphin, Gun Garden

1710–1717	Bethia Hayden
1722	John Charles
1729–1740	George Ogley
1740	Ann Ogley
1740–1753	Thomas Beane
1753–1766	Anne Beane

1766–1768	John Beane
1768–1770	Richard Breeds
1771	Thomas Wherwell
1772–1801	James Hook
1801	(closed)

Ferry Boat (1),
| 1735 | William Curtis |

Ferry Boat (2), Ferry Road
1838–1839	Thomas Jarrett
1845	John Earle
1852–1863	James Glazier
1863–1865	John Almond
1866–1874	Henry Jempson
1878–1886	Diana Jempson
1890–1893	William Foster
1894	Joseph Ridley
1894–1895	Henry James
1895	Ernest Trill
1898	James Jennings (**New Inn**)
1899	William Thomas Bourn
1899–1900	Thomas Waite
1900–1913	John H Paine
1913–1915	Charles E Preece
1915	Henry Chapman
1915–1930	Henry Bennett
1930–1938	Walter Jerrard
1940	Ruth Timmins
1960 (?)	(**Ferry Boat**)
1968	Raymond Fry

Flushing Inn, Market Street
1739–1750	John Igglesden
1750–1751	William Marchant
1751	(closed)
1915	(**Old Flushing Inn Fresco Club**)
1960–2010	Mann/Flynn family
2010	(closed)

Foresters, Mint
| 1826–1832 | Richard Heath (**Dolphin**) |

1839	Charles Poole/Poile
1845	Edward Standen
1852–1853	Samuel Knight
1853	Henry Hurst
1853–1854	Edward Edwards
1856	Edwin James
1856	Thomas Shearer
1858–1861	William Allan
1861–1865	Edwin Pulford
1865	Rodmond Chatterton **(Foresters)**
1868–1870	Richard Prior
1870	Sara Stone
1873	William Stone
1873–1879	Robert Button
1879–1881	Jessie Cousins
1881	Samuel Chapman (brewery agent)
1881–1894	Barnabas Taylor
1894–1895	William Watts
1895	Barnabas Taylor
1896–1902	Edward Lambert
1902–1903	Henry J Jones
1903–1905	David Barry
1906	Alfred Skinner
1906	(closed)

Fortune

1754	Thomas Ward
1758	

George Inn, High Street

1575	Edward Bryan
1648	William Coaker
1670	John Prowse
1670	John Crouch
1707	John Carr
1709	John Russell
1722	Giles Palmer
1724–1725	William Bird
1731	Wiltshire Slade
1736–1752	Michael Woollett
1753–1756	William Cooper
1756–1761	Thomas Hovenden

1761–1771	John Laurence
1777	William Brooman
1779–1793	Despar Rummins
1793–1794	James Elliot
1794–1796	Richard Tutt
1796–1799	Thomas Stockwell
1800–1803	William Mayo
1804–1806	John Blake
1806–1808	James Rogers
1808–1829	Thomas Godfrey
1829–1834	Joseph Hollyer
1838	Trayton Poole
1839–1840	John Meryon
1845	Harriet Hilder
1852–1858	George Hilder
1859–1862	Frederick King
1862–1874	Richard Smith
1877–1901	William Cowtan
1901–1914	Henry F Weale
1914–1915	Ada Hall
	William Williams (secretary of Mackeson Ltd)
1918–1925	Walter Wood
1930–1940	Annie Wood
1940	Charles Forte

George Tap/Bar, Lion Street

1767	Edward Sayers
1858	Ann Carsons
1866	Henry Huckstepp
1872	Thomas Apps
1899	Frederick King

Globe, Military Road

1834–1840	John Wheeler
1840	Thomas Harmer
1852–1858	James Dunk
1859–1899	Marshall Ames
1899–1902	Emily Ames (daughter)
1903–1906	Edwin J Roberts
1906–1908	Charles Brown
1908	George Lambert
1908–1911	George Eaton

1911–1915	Benjamin Thomas
1918–1933	George Eaton
1934	Richard Barry
1938–1940	S Tullett

Greyhound, Wish Street

1844	Elizabeth Barham
1845	James Hedgecock
1852–1863	John Myers
1864–1873	Charles Jempson
1873–1882	John Ball
1885	Mr Taylor
1882–1887	Thomas Hubbard
1888–1894	Rebecca Hubbard
1894	Rebecca Stocks (formerly Hubbard)
1895	Albert Stocks
1896–1903	Charles Masters
1904–1905	Robert Mann
1905	Thomas Mannering
1905	Percival Flynn
1906	Frank Bryant
1906	(closed)

Hope and Anchor, Watchbell Street

1838	
1849–1853	Edward Fowle
1855	Edward Spicer
1856–1858	Isaac Wright
1859	Richard Wood
1859	Samuel Chapman (brewery agent)
1860	Edward Fowle
1862	Samuel Chapman (brewery agent)
1862	Theophulus Fuggle
1863	Mary Collins
1864	(closed 'for a considerable time')
1865–1873	Eliza Wallis
1875	Daniel Brett
1875–1878	Charles Catt
1878–1879	Edward Skinner
1879	Mrs Skinner
1879	Nathanial King
1881	Henry Button

1881–1889	George Knight
1890–1899	Mary Elizabeth Knight
1899	Maria Coleman
1905–1907	Esther Fearn
19??–1911	William Bradley
1911–1914	Eliza F Bradley
1915	George Parkes-Wood (brewery agent
1915–1916	George H Coulson
1916–1918	George Parkes-Wood (brewery agent)
1922	William H Best
1925	(closed)
1925–1934	Miss C Bellrose (reopened as a hotel)

Hope & Anchor BH, Watchbell Street
1838	William Woolett
1862	Edwin Swaddling
1873–1875	Stephen Smith

Hoy
1757

Jolly Sailor, Watchbell Street
1830–1839	Thomas Hearsfield
1839–1841	Mary Hearsfield
1841–1874	James Dawson
1874–1886	William Watts
1886–1891	George Marsh
1891–1893	Thomas Clark
1893	Harriet Clarke (widow)
1893	Harriet Green
1893–1894	George Green
1894	John Bowen (brewery agent)
1899–1902	Henry Wilson
1902–1904	Edwin Best
1904–1907	William Bartlett
1907–1909	Albert Perrin
1909	John Best
1911	(closed)

Kings Arms, Cinque Ports Street
early 1830	Thomas Aylward (**William the Fourth**)
1838	Samuel Austin

1838	Thomas Aylward
1838–1844	George Whiteman
1845	Thomas Marshall
1852–1859	James Hobbs Star
1860–1870	George Whiteman
1873	William Dixon
1873	Mr Humber
1873–1874	Charles Boulter
1878–1881	Henry John Jarrett
1881–1884	Peter Morris (**Kings Arms**)
1884–1885	William Bailey
1885–1886	William Mills
1887	George Eldridge (brewery agent)
1887	Frank Weatherman
1890–1895	Henry Elliott
1897–1909	Moses Hoad
1909	(closed)

Kings Arms (2)

| 1722 | James Grayward |

Kings Head, Rye Hill

Lamb, Tower Street

| 1838–1839 | William Neeves |
| 1845 | Alfred Marley |

London Stout House BH (Ferry Road)

1852–1870	Henry Huggett (**Huggett's Beer House**)
1870	William Stone
1873	John Ball
1873–1875	John Jarrett (**Two Sawyers**)
1875	Richard Balcombe
1875–1878	William Watson
1878–1881	James Porter
1881–1892	George Tedham
1892–1900	Frederick Bryant (**London Stout House**)
1900	Herbert Buckland
1900–1901	William Pope
1901	Frank Bryant
1902–1903	Amos Bannister
1903–1907	George Donovan

1908	William Leggett
1908	(closed)

Maypole
1707

Mermaid, Mermaid Street

1536	Richard Pedyll
1588	William Didsbury
1600s	Thomas Higgons
1634–1638	William Gostree
1652	Michael Cadman
1716–1724	William Bird
1724–1735	Thomas Bean
1742–1746	William Rockett
1746–1750	John Goddon
1750	(closed)
1894	(Re-opened as a private hotel incorporating Mermaid Club)
1948	Lawrence Wilson
1955	William Holden

Morphotes Tippling House, Strand

Oak, 106–107 High Street

1859	William Fuggle? **(Pig & Whistle)**
1867–1870	Alfred Bourn
1878–1881	Francis Barden
1881–1892	Thomas Osborne (**Oak**)
1892	Mrs Osborne
1893	Alfred Butcher
1893–1895	Stephen Irvine
1895–1896	Sarah Irvine
1896–1899	Charles Ditcher
1899	Arthur Page
1899	Albert Pentecost
1900–1909	George Collyer
1910	(closed)

Old Bell, The Mint

1845	Samuel Thompson
1849–1862	Elizabeth Paine
1865–1870	Mary Sheather

1878	Mary Ann Samson
1878	George Avenden
1882–1883	Mary Wickenden
1883	Frederick Wickenden
1890–1899	Charles Fletcher
1902–1922	Lawrence Seers
1927	Louisa Seers
1930–1940	Leslie Fletcher
1968	Frederick Battley

Pipemakers Arms, Wish Street

1830–1834?	Richard Cogger (**BH**)
1834–1838	Anne Cogger?
1844	William Augustus Walker
1852	William Bourn (1)
1863–1866	William Bourn (2)
1867	Ann Bourn
1870	James Ashdown
1870–1890	William Fairhall
1891–1895	George Killick
1895	J Bowen (brewery agent)
1895–1898	George Coleburne
1898	James Burt
1901	George Parkes Wood (brewery agent)
1901–1903	Alfred Marsh
1903	Sarah Marsh
1903–1927	Thomas W Martin
1930–1940	Charles Killick

Ports Arms

| 1722 | Thomas Cooper |

Prince of Orange
1707

Queen Adelaide, Ferry Road

1832–1837	Alexander Sinclair
1838–1840	James Phillips
1845–1851	Peter Pankhurst
1852	Mr Nash
1859–1862	William Roof
1862	Phoebe Ashton

1862	Joseph Webster
1863	Martha Warren
1864–1899	William Warren
1900–1901	William Southby
1901	John Tampkin
1902	Harry Tibbles
1902–1916	Edward Craig
1916–1918	Emma Craig
1918–1925	Edward Craig
1925–1933	Emma Craig
1934–1940	A E Jamieson

Queen's Arms, 7–9 West Street/Middle Street?

1655	
1722	Richard Fowls

Queens Head, Landgate

1722	Edward Nightingale (**Two Brewers**)
1735–1746	John Dowdy
1746–1751	Elizabeth Dowdy
1751–1759	Elizabeth Bray
1759–1764	John Haddock
1764–1768	Richard Breads
1768–1777	Robert Cloake/Clarke
1777–1778	Sharrington Russell
1778–1781	John Hunter (**Queens Head**)
1782–1788	Cornelius Kemp
1789–1794	John Pilcher
1795–1796	James Cochran
1796–1797	John Smith
1797–1798	Mary Smith
1799	Stephen Epps
1800–1817	John Norley
1825	John Garrett
1826	Elizabeth Garrett
1824–1826	Thomas Crowhurst
1832–1834	William Woolett
1838	Edwin Turk
1839	Thomas Phillips
1845	John Ditton
1852	William Norley
1858–1884	William Elliot

1884–1888	Obed Waghorn
1888–1891	William Henry Moore
1891–1892	Richard Gain
1893–1895	George Elliott
1895–1899	Alfred Greysmith
1899	Albert Wilden
1902–1905	Charles Hopperton
1905–1907	Thomas Kerwin
1907–1908	Arthur Hill
1908–1930	Richard D McKenzie
1932–1934	George Edmed
1938	Edwin G Terry
1940	Gordon Terry
1969	Adam Banks

Red Lion, Lion Street

1574	
1710	Thomas Kyd
1714	Alice Kyd
1717–1735	John Beaver
1735–1738	Widow Beaver
1739–1742	Henry Thorowgood
1742–1756	Robert Cooper
1756–1757	Thomas Edwards
1757–1777	Thomas Woollett
1777–1781	James Elliott
1781–1784	John Pilcher
1784–1788	Charles Pilcher
1788–1791	Wade Reynold Pollet
1791–1798	Robert Eason
1798–1800	George Mugglestone
1801–1802	John Hughes
1802–1809	Thomas Skinner
1810–1825	William Woollet
1825–1826	Stephen Kennett
1832–1839	Edwin Hilder
1845	Edgar Brignall
1852–1862	Richard Smith
1862	William Bowra
1862–1866	John Reed
1867	Richard Chapman
1867	William Piper

| 1868 | Shearer |
| 1868–1872 | Frank Hemmings |

Red Cross
1722

Royal Oak, Hilders Cliff
17th century

Rye Galley, Tower Street
| 1739–1777 | John Bean |
| 1777–1780 | Sarah Bean |

Ship, Strand
1836–1839	James Crowhurst
1839	George Thomas
1841–1851	John Christmas
1851–1858	John Ditton
1858	George Whiteman
1859–1860	James Nye
1860	Mr Catt
1862	Eliza Flannighan
1862	Mr Medhurst
1863	Alice Bowden
1864	Mary Prior
1866	R Prior
1869	James Osborne
1870–1876	Thomas Osborne
1876	George Skinner
1878–1879	Thomas Riddle
1882–1884	Charles Peppett
1884–1885	Richard Johnson
1885	Henry Jarrett
1886–1887	Thomas Russell London
1887–1888	Joseph Bayley
1888	John Piper
1889–1890	William Mason
1891–1892	George Page
1892–1895	Frederick Page
1892	Robert John London
1895–1909	James Collins
1909–1910	John Coote

1910	B Burtonshaw
1913–1922	Edward McEntee
1930–1932	Thomas Neeves
1935–1938	Frederick Foord
1938–1940	Albert E Bryan
1971–1973	Michael Kennard

Ship in Distress, Tower Street

1709	
1767	Mr Honis

Shipp (without Landgate)

1720s	
1722	Mary Powell (widow)
1735	Richard Paris
1745	Dame Paris

Sims BH, Strand

1883	George Sims

Standard, Mint

1863–1870	Alfred Jarrett
1874–1879	William Woolett
1879	Edwin Finn
1879–1882	William Jarrett
1882–1891	Thomas Field
1891–1893	Samuel Sandells
1893–1907	William Foster
1913–1922	Charles Standing
1926	Ernest Martin
1927	G Farthing
1930–1940	Albert Harrison
1938–1940	Charles Olley
1940	Arthur Eastwood
1940–1946	Edith Eastwood
1946	Arthur Eastwood

Swan, The Butchery

1581	Edward Call

Swan Inn, Mint

1860?–1864	John Holt

1864	William Watson
1864–1868	Henry Francis
1869–1870	Richard Cole
1872	Charles Wilding
1873	Henry Francis
1874	Henry Cloke
1878	William Moore
1881	Mrs Moore
1881	Edwin Finn (brewery agent)
1882	David Ben Dann
1885	Charles Woolett
1885–1888	Richard Johnson
1888–1898	William Axell
1899–1906	Edward Brown
1906	(closed)

Three Kings, Middle Street (Mermaid Street)
| 1576 | |
| 1590 | John Fisher |

Three Mariners, 15 High Street
| 1592 | Agnes Tokey |

Tower, Landgate
1845–1862	Robert Dunk
1866–1870	William Mills
1874	Thomas Jordon
1878–1888	Thomas Dale
1890–1911	James Taylor
1911	(closed)

Union, East Street
1831–1838	John Hunter
1839	Sarah Hunter
1852–1861	James Hunter
1861	John Munn
1863	George Peake
1863	Mr Baldwin
1864	George Austin
1864	Henry Huckstepp
1866	C Dann
1888–1892	George Elliott

1892–1894	Maria Coleman
1894	William Richardson
1898	Ernest Hyland
1898–1899	Alfred Ashdown
1900	Henry Hawkins
1900–1934	Frederick C Bryant
1940	J G Carruthers

White Vine, High Street

Ypres Castle Inn, Gun Garden

1839	George French
1852	William Watson
1859–1861	Eliza Ashton
1861–1863	William Bourn
1864	Miss Bourn (daughter)
1865	John Hyder
1873	William Dixon?
1865–1893	Richard Adams
1893–1903	Frank Francis
1903–1904	George Coote
1904	Alfred Gall
1907–1909	Richard Cockett
1909	Mrs Cockett
1909–1932	Thomas Neeves
1927	Elizabeth Richardson
1930–1934	Elizabeth Harriet Hickling
1938–1940	Thomas A Bullen
1940–1943	Valentine Francis
1943	Walter Bray

APPENDIX 2
Rye Friendly Societies

The earliest benefit society in Rye was the Rye Benefit Society, which in 1762 loaned £80 to the churchwardens. By the next century there were many such societies, including the Wellington Lodge of Freemasons, formed in 1814. The six principle societies were:

The Rye Ancient Towns' Friendly Society: founded in 1828 at the London Trader. 'Twice dissolved and funds shared out.' It later moved to the Cinque Ports Arms.

The Court Friars Foresters: founded in 1853 at the New Inn, Winchelsea. It moved to the Cinque Ports Arms in 1855 and then to the Coffee Tavern in 1896 with 80 members.

The Court Harold Foresters: founded at the London Trader in 1855 and moved to the Red Lion in about 1860. After the fire in 1872 it moved to the Queen's Head and then to the Coffee Tavern in 1888.

The Prince of Wales Lodge of Oddfellows: founded at the London Trader in 1842. It met at the Red Lion from 1860 until 1872 then moved to the Coffee Tavern in 1888.

The Phoenix Lodge of Oddfellows: founded at the Cinque Ports Arms in 1823. It met in the Red Lion from 1860.

The Amicable Mariners: founded in 1844 at the Hope and Anchor and moved to the Crown in 1856.

All these societies provided sickness benefit and the services of a doctor. Indeed they were the major employer of the town's doctors in the 19th century. They also provided annuities, death benefits and social activities. The most important day in their calendar was Rye Gala Day in July.

Report of Gala Day, 1870:

Grand Union Festival of the Rye Friendly Societies.
The Rye Ancient Towns Friendly Benefit Society; the Prince of Wales
Lodge off Odd. Fellows M.U.; the Friars and Harold Courts of
Foresters; and the Phoenix Lodge of Odd Fellows, will hold their
Anniversaries on TUESDAY JULY 12th, 1870, when they will
meet at the Queens Head, Landgate, at 9.45 a.m., and at 10 o'clock
attend Divine Service at the Parish Church. At 11 o'clock
the members will assemble at their various club houses, and
afterwards unite in a
GRAND PROCESSION!
Headed by the SPLENDID BAND OF THE EAST KENT
MILITIA, (under the able direction of Bandmaster Wood), and parade
the principal streets of the Town, accompanied by
THREE SUPERIOR BANDS OF MUSIC
And the Banners, Flags, and Regalia of the different Orders,
returning to their respective club houses. The Members of Court
Friars, A.O.F. will dine together at the Cinque Ports Hotel, tickets
3s. each. The Prince of Wales Lodge, M.U., and Friendly Society,
will dine in a large Marquee adjoining the Globe Inn, where dinner
will be provided by Bro. Marshall Ames. Tickets 2s. 6d. each. The
Court Harold, A.O.F., and the Phoenix Lodge of Odd Fellows will
dine together at the Red Lion Inn, tickets 3s. each. The Amicable
Mariners will dine at the Crown Inn.
A GRAND FETE CHAMPETRE!
Will take place in the beautiful grounds of Mountsfield. At three o'clock
the usual variety of Games, Sports, &c. will be provided. Splendid
Brass Bands and a Quadrille Band will be engaged for the occasion.
IMMENSE ATTRACTIONS! *will be introduced.*
The Great ETHERDO, the Equilibrium Wonder, Favourite Clown,
and Italian Jaggier on the Slack Wire. Madame EL NEMO HUME
on the Invisible Wire; this lady's wonderful performance must be
seen to be believed. The extraordinary Comic and Eccentric Dancer,
PETA BELTON, in his unrivalled feats. Mr. and Mrs. TOM
ARNOLD, sensation duettists, comic and serio-comic singers. Miss
NELLY ASHTON, characteristic singer and dancer, will give
her ideas on the times in general. Mr. SAM DUDLEY,
comedian and champion big-boot dancer. A Magic Post Office,
together with other novelties.
There will be a Magnificent Display of
FIREWORKS AND BALLOONS
In the Evening, on a more Extensive Scale, and far superior to any
former Exhibition in Rye and an Illumination by means of the
MAGNESIUM LIGHT.

During the 1860s the societies were united, and nearly always marched together under a joint committee. For several years they dined together in marquees erected on the Red Lion Bowling Green Arbour, the Cinque Ports Rose Garden, on the Salts, or in their lodges. Because they met in public houses, the societies were a target of the temperance lobby from the late 1860s.

A temperance letter submitted to the press in 1862 stated that 'most friendly societies still hold their meetings in public houses, with landlords for treasurers; and the members are required by the rules to spend a monthly sum in beer "for the good of the house", which amount is taken from the box, whether the members have or have not paid their contributions, and in many instances the money is not repaid to the society.' However, there is no evidence for this assertion.

In 1870 a difference of opinion between Foresters and temperance campaigners came to a head. A meeting in the Cinque Ports Arms, called to decide on whether the Foresters should move out of the pub and hold their meetings in unlicensed premises, was disrupted when their chairman said he had been: "grossly insulted by the temperance lobby". He vacated the chair and spent the evening in the bar. "As to the morality of holding meetings in the Cinque Ports Arms", he said, "many members would not attend the club if they could not enjoy a pipe and a glass of beer". However, the Court Friars continued meeting in the Cinque Ports Arms for another 26 years.

In 1888 the Rye Coffee Tavern Co formerly offered the use of its premises in the High Street to the Friendly Societies. The offer was accepted by the Prince of Wales Oddfellows.

This was followed by 'a special meeting of Court Harold, Foresters held at the Queens Head, Landgate, where it was resolved, by 67 to 39 votes, to change the headquarters of the club to the Rye Coffee Tavern, High Street ie provided the directors enlarge their Assembly Room, which, we believe is in contemplation. Two of the leading societies have now given preference to the temperance house, and it remains to be seen whether the other two will move in the same direction.'

In 1896 the Rye Philanthropic Society was founded at the Queens Head, which also hosted the Rye Lodge of Buffaloes. In the same year, Court Friars Foresters held their last meeting in the Cinque Ports Arms:

Bro. Charles Fletcher, one of the oldest members of the Lodge, delivered an address during the evening, in the course of which he said that several of the old members regarded the decision of the majority to move the headquarters to the Temperance Hotel as something approaching a mistake, although they loyally bowed, to the feeling that had been expressed. As far as himself was concerned, he had spent many pleasant evenings under that roof since he had become a member of the Court, now some 40 years ago. (Applause.) His recollection, therefore, went back over a considerable period of the Committee's history, and he could not help saying that the meetings which had been held in bygone years had been very much better attended than those of recent date, for in the old days there was a genuine fraternal feeling, which pervaded the whole of the business....

Apparently the feeling which now existed among some of the members was that they ought to look at their business in a more serious light, and they might possibly be so impressed with that seriousness which induced them to sit round the table with faces as solemn as judges. (Laughter.) At the same time, he thought it would be better if a more pleasant feeling existed amongst them. If they acted up to their rules and precepts, giving each other no opportunity in fault-finding, he believed it would be of great assistance to the Court in obtaining an increase of membership, in adding to its influence, and in enabling it to take a proper position in the town. During the 40 years of which he had spoken he had seen many changes and vicissitudes but he did not intend to become the reminiscent. He could not help, however, referring to the fact that many of the old familiar faces had passed away – members who always met with the most pleasant feelings, and encouraged mutual respect and goodwill.

At the turn of the century the first of many slate clubs was established at the New Inn, Ferry Road and by the First World War several friendly societies had gone into abeyance because of bad management and investment. They were replaced by 14 slate clubs meeting in public houses, including four women only branches. By 1940 these were held at the:- Bedford, Crown, Globe, New Inn, Olde Bell, Pipemakers, Queen Adelaide, Standard, Ship and Ypres Castle. Women only branches met at the Olde Bell, Pipemakers, Queen Adelaide and the Ship. In addition each of these pubs also had a birthday club.

There was also a Thrift Club at the Queens Head, the Tunbridge Wells Equitable Friendly Society at the Crown, and the Social Brothers Benefit Society at the Standard. The Foresters and Oddfellows still functioned but now met in the Congregational Schools.

APPENDIX 3
Rye Temperance Movement

The Rye temperance movement existed for over a century until the 1930s. It was never a single united organisation but a lobby group made up of several different strands.

Temperance first appeared in Rye in the 1830s in response to a national call for 'abstinence from alcohol' by people calling themselves 'teetotallers'. Teetotallers were a hard, extreme group who campaigned for prohibition, the closure of all licensed premises, and for alcohol to be made illegal. Their main organisation in Rye was the International Order of Good Templars who had two local branches. In the 1860s they were joined by the Baptists, Quakers and the Salvation Army.

A second religious strand was pursued by those who saw themselves as missionaries. They included, for example, the Band of Hope (1853) who wanted to 'rescue children from the perils of drink', and the Rye Temperance Society (1855), who claimed in 1865 that 762 adults and children had signed the pledge. Their stated aim was 'to snatch drunkards from a miserable life, a hopeless death and a wretched eternity'.

A third group was the Church of England Temperance Society (CETS), which had at least two Rye branches by the 1870s. The society, known as 'moral suasionst', attempted to recruit drinkers, and persuade them to moderate their drinking but not necessarily give up — see the Pipemakers Arms and the Cinque Ports Assembly Rooms. CETS was criticised by the 'teetotallers' who claimed that 'moderation keeps the publican in business'.

Yet another group in Rye were those who also wanted to moderate consumption, but believed that alcohol had medicinal properties. Towards the end of the 19th century when liquor consumption was falling, local breweries supported this idea with early forms of marketing. The George advertisement for Milk Stout is a good example.

From about 1870, Rye temperance campaigners within the Friendly Societies, attempted to persuade Friendly Societies to stop meeting in public houses. They had some success when the Harold Lodge and Friars Lodge of the Foresters moved from the Queens Head in 1888, and from the Cinque Ports Arms in 1896 respectively. Both Lodges moved into the Rye Coffee Tavern.

THE

RYE COFFEE TAVERN

Nos. 8 & 9, HIGH STREET

(Top of Conduit Hill).

RYE, ☦ SUSSEX.

COMMERCIAL, COFFEE, READING, AND PRIVATE ROOMS.

Every Accommodation for Commercials, Tourists, Cyclists, & Others.

⁎ HOT DINNERS ⁎

FROM 12 TILL 2.

Tea, Coffee, & Cocoa always ready.

EXCURSIONISTS PROVIDED FOR IN LARGE OR SMALL PARTIES.

⁎ GOOD AND WELL-AIRED BEDS. ⁎

The Rye Coffee Tavern opened in 1881 'in opposition to secret tippling' but found the temperance market limited. Also the Warden Temperance Hotel found it difficult to get custom. Before the First World War the chairman, Cllr J Deacon, remarked: "In 1898 we owed £500 and thought of winding up. It was not until 1914 that we paid any dividend. It has been a long and trying experience."

The Temperance Lobby also responded to many single issues including Sunday Closing in 1879, and the Local Veto Bill in 1908, when large numbers of Rye publicans and their customers, carrying bunches of hops, marched against this bill in London. The Local Veto Bill was soon abandoned.

There was a gender dimension of temperance when the British Women's Temperance Society (BWTA), Rye branch, set up in 1907. Many, if not most temperance campaigners were women, and the BWTA was bent on persuading men to stop drinking and spending a large share of the household income on drink.

After the First World War 'total abstinence' and prohibition started to decline, and a new, less emotional temperance movement emerged in an attempt to 'reform' the public house.

At this time the Union Inn, East Street, became a 'Goth pub' when it was acquired by the People's Refreshment House Association Ltd. This was a temperance organisation influenced by the 'Gothenburg Model of disinterested management' founded in Sweden. The manager of the Union was described as an 'agent in the cause of temperance and good behaviour', was paid a fixed salary, plus any profit from food and non-alcoholic drinks. All profit from alcohol was donated to local 'objects of public utility'. A few 'Goth pubs' still exist in Scotland but as far as is known the Union was the only one in Rye.

Also in the 1930s, a booklet: *Some British Inns. No 2: The Mermaid Rye,* by local author A G Bradley, was published by the

True Temperance Association (see the Mermaid). But this was a confused organisation very different from any of the early campaigns and without clear aims.

Warden Temperance Hotel, late 19th century

APPENDIX 4
The Treating Scandal 1852

H P Clark describes a scene which occurred during the canvass and General Election of 1852. 'Public-houses were opened free to all, and the scenes of dissipation were disgraceful; yet the candidate, like all others, declared that he was a protestant and a supporter of religion. There were men and women, boys and girls, drunk. Some were brawling drunk, some crying drunk, some singing drunk, some fighting drunk, some stupid drunk, some cunning drunk, some crazy drunk, and some drunk.'

The following is a list of the public houses and beer houses at which treating took place between the 1st June and 1st August 1852. The source of this list is the parliamentary report from the Select Committee 1853.

NAME OF HOUSES	LANDLORD		£. s. d.	£. s. d.
Red Lion	Richard Smith	21 June	8 9 3	
		July	16 14 -	
			13 13 10	
			16 10 2	
			11 15 -	
		Polling return	101 - -	
		Together		168 2 3
George	George Hilder	June	4 2 6	
		Return	60 - -	
				64 2 6
Cinque Ports	Charles Paul	20 June	4 7 6	
Queen's Head	William Norley	25 June	12 10 -	
		July	17 13 6	
		August	5 - 10	
				35 4 4
Horse and Groom	William Richardson	15 June	1 7 3	
		19 June (band)	3 12 -	
		21 June	6 3 -	

			£	s	d	£	s	d
		3 bills	30	9	9			
						41	12	-
King William the Fourth	James Hobbs Starr	19 June	3	12	-			
		June	6	10	-			
		Aug Polling day, per Aylward	45	15	-			
						55	17	-
Hope and Anchor	Edward Fowle	24 June	8	4	6			
		August	13	18	6			
						22	3	-
Tower	Robert Dunk	15 June	-	12	6			
		19 June	3	12	-			
		26 June	10	7	6			
						24	12	-
Ypres Castle	William Watson	19 June	3	12	-			
		July	12	15	6			
						16	7	6
King's Head	George Allaway	19 June	3	12	-			
		28 June	4	15	-			
		July	8	15	-			
		Polling-day	40	-	-			
						57	2	-
Globe	Jane Dunk	19 June	4	-	-			
		August	-	13	6			
		August	2	1	6			
						6	15	-
Pipemakers' Arms	William Bourn	19 June	3	12	-			
		June	8	18	-			
		July	8	1	-			
						20	11	-
Greyhound	John Myers	19 June	3	12	-			
		July	10	16	6			
		August	10	1	11			
						24	10	5
White Swan	William Betts	19 June	4	-	-			
		July	5	15	-			
		August	2	14	-			
						12	9	-
Hare and Hounds	Robert Barnes	July	18	16				
						18	16	-
Beer-shop	Henry Huggett	19 June	3	12	-			
		July	12	15	-			
		August	2	10	-			
						18	17	-
Jolly Sailors	James Dawson	19 June	3	12	-			
		July	7	1	6			
		August	4	12	-			
						15	15	6
Castle, (Winchelsea)	Richard Osborne	19 June	10	1	6			
		July	59	8	6			
		Polling-day	21	-	-			

Establishment	Name	Date	£	s	d	£	s	d
						90	10	-
New Inn (Winchelsea)	Jane Harrod	July	13	8	-	13	8	-
Cock (Peasmarsh)	Edward Paine	June	29	15	6			
		August, per Aylward Polling-day	26	10	-			
						56	5	6
Ferry Boat	James Glazier	19 June	3	12	-			
		July	9	16	-			
						13	8	-
Old Bell	Elizabeth Paine	19 June	3	12	-			
						3	12	-
London Trader	George Austin	19 June	3	12	-			
						3	12	-
Beer-shop, Peasmarsh	Edward Bannister	June	3	12	-			
		July	14	17	6			
						18	9	6
Robin Hood (Ick)	John Overy	July	41	-	-			
						41	-	-
Beer-shop	William Hovendon	June	13	10	-			
		July	7	4	-			
		July	2	8	-			
						23	2	-
	In List Delivered					899	4	-
19 June	Ship, Ditton's at Harbour		8	8	-			
	Queen Adelaide, Nash		3	12	-			
	Dolphin, Knight		3	12	-			
	Nye's Beer-shop		3	12	-			
						19	4	-
June	Child's Eating-house		3	12	-			
July	ditto		9	3	-			
August	ditto		2	12	-			
						15	7	-
						934	15	-
	S. Fryman, Wine-Merchant							
June	Bill		20	2	6			
July	ditto		92	5	-			
August	ditto		5	-	-			
						117	7	6
						1,052	2	6
	Supper at Pipemakers' Arms to Cook's party					1	10	-
						1,053	12	6

APPENDIX 5
Mock Mayor Elections

The 'election' of a mock mayor about Landgate seems to have taken place in Rye every year from 1825 until about 1870. H P Clark, writing in his *Guide and History of Rye* (1861) when the tradition was still alive, recalled that: 'In the early part of the present century a few of the inhabitants of Landgate, who by the Corporation were designated Jacobins, what now would be called Radical Reformers, by way of derision elected a mayor for that part of the town, and so they continue yearly.'

Much interest, both local and national, was caused in 1825 when John Meryon was 'elected' as a 'rebel' Mayor of Rye, in opposition to the legal Mayor, Dr. Lamb. Headlines about the Town with Two Mayors blazed on the front pages of every national newspaper and eventually the law had to be called in to depose the rebel mayor and his corporation, who had established themselves in the Town Hall.

At 12 noon on the 9th November each year at the Town Hall the Mayor of the Borough was elected, this was the official Mayor. But later in the day, around 6.0'clock, the Mayor of Landgate was nominated by the tradesmen and fishermen. The Mayor-without-the Borough, as he was called, was initiated at the Queens Head.

And in 1859:-

The Freemen of this part of the Borough assembled at the Court Hall, Queens Head on Wednesday evening last, according to their annual custom, for the purpose of electing a Mayor. After partaking of a sumptuous supper of red herrings, which were served in a first-rate style by Mr. Elliott, the important business of the meeting commenced.

William Paine, Mayor of Landgate, 1859

The three Candidates nominated for the office were — Mr. William Paine, cordwainer, who has filled the civic chair for many years, and for whom 18 votes were recorded, Mr. John Wheeler, gentleman, for whom 8 votes were given; and Mr. Michael Martin, mason, who was honoured by receiving 7 votes. The election was therefore declared to have fallen upon Mr. Paine, who was duly installed into the dignities of the office.

The next business was that of electing a Town Clerk; Mr. Stephen Lindridge being the only candidate, he was declared to be duly elected. Mr. James Vennall was appointed town crier and bill poster, and Parker Butcher and Henry Wood, constables without salaries.

After various minor matters were disposed of, the business was declared to be at an end, and the company proceeded to indulge in their glass of grog with pipe and song, passing the evening with the greatest hilarity and good feeling. We ought not to omit to state that a very handsome pair of maces were provided for the occasion; some wag has informed us that the maces consisted of two enormous pumpkins, but we cannot believe that an affair which was carried on with so much spirit would in the end prove 'seedy'.

In 1864 the 'maces' were in the hands of the Amicable Mariners Benefit Society, who carried them in the Rye Gala Day procession of that year. The Amicable Mariners were based at the Crown Inn, and a late attempt by them to elect a 'Landgate mayor' took place in the Crown in 1874. This meeting was described by the local press as a 'farcical ceremony'.

A final reference to 'Landgate Mayoring' is recorded as late as 1896. In that year the Rye Philanthropic Society was founded at the Queens Head and held its inaugural meeting there in October. One speaker remarked that: "The occasion brings to mind some of the old associations when Landgate had a mayor of its own." At that point the ancient maces attaching to the office of Mayor of Landgate were brought into the room amid much applause.

NOTICE to the BURGESSES.

On Thursday November the 9th 1854,
WILLIAM PAINE, Esquire,
was duly Elected to the office of

MAYOR,

For the Borough of Landgate, Rye.

E. EASTON, Esq., Deputy Mayor.

H. Killick,
W. Relf, } Esqs., **ALDERMEN.**

Messrs. E. Clark,
T. Gilbert,
W. Chrowhurst,
J. Smith,
W. King,
W. Waters. } **COUNCILLORS.**

G. TRICE, Esq., Clerk.

At the Inauguration the Worshipfull the Mayor delivered the following address.

Gentlemen,

I thank you all kindly for the high honour that you have this day conferred upon me, by electing me as your Mayor for this Borough; and, during my mayoralty I will endeavour to remove all nuisances, redress all grievances, promote the interest and welfare of the Borough at large, and will be ready at all times to attend to any duty that may devolve upon me. I hope that the bloody war will soon end, then, and not till then, we may expect better times. Gentlemen, I thank you for the attention you have paid during my arraign, and I wish prosperity and happiness to you all.

[H. P. CLARK, Printer to the Corporative Body.]

Reference Notes

The following abbreviations are used in the reference notes:

RC   *Rye Chronicle*
SE Ad   *South Eastern Advertiser*
SE   *Sussex Express*
SWA   *Sussex Weekly Advertiser*

All other references are as written or refer to the National Archive.

Bedford Arms
1 AMS 5681/30/6
2 op cit
3 Rye/70/35
4 RC 15/10/1870
5 SE Ad 24/02/1910
6 SE 3/09/1948
7 SE 8/02/1946

Borough Arms
1 SE Ad 20/02/1875
2 SE Ad 27/02/1875
3 SE Ad 26/08/1893
4 SE Ad 10/03/1906
5 SE Ad 7/03/1906
6 SE Ad 12/7/1907

Bull Head
1 DAP 103/3
2 DAP 155
3 DAP 51/1
4 Rye/14/21/c-d
5 Rye/70/33
6 Holloway 1847, p438
7 SWA 18/10/1756
8 Russell 10/2011

Cinque Ports Arms
1 SE 3/06/1837
2 SE Ad 24/04/1875

Cinque Ports Assembly Room
1 *Rye Memories* vol 2, p102
2 SE Ad 11/02/1905
3 SE Ad 2/12/1899
4 SE Ad 25/02/1905
5 SE Ad 17/05/1913
6 SE Ad 23/3/1913
7 SE Ad 19/12/1914
8 SE Ad 16/10/1915
9 SE 15/03/1948
10 SE 16/6/1972

Cinque Ports (Railway)
1 RC 14/02/1867
2 VID/2/2/69
3 SE Ad 11/04/1885
4 SE Ad 23/11/1907
5 Russell 10/2011
6 VID/5/29/1-4

Crown
1 SE Ad 16/08/1879
2 SE Ad 26/01/1860
3 SE Ad 28/05/1881
4 RC 4/07/1874
5 SE 17/01/1947

3 SE Ad 25/01/1879
4 SE Ad 24/02/1883
5 PAB 325/2

Dial
1 AMS 5681/74/1
2 op cit
3 *London Gazette* 1849
4 AMS 5681/74/
5 RC 29/08/1863, 27/08/1864
6 AMS 5681/74/4-5
7 AMS 5681/74/6
8 *Rye Memories* vol 13, p68

Dolphin
1 Rye/7/30
2 Rye/7/31
3 Rye/142/16
4 Rye/142/11

Ferry Boat Inn
1 Rye 14/21b
2 Rye 14/21c-d
3 AMS 5681/30
4 AMS 6128/29
5 RC 25.02/1865
6 SE Ad 2/07/1898
7 SE Ad 7/01/1899
8 *Adams Guide to Rye* 1934
9 *Rye's Own vol 8, no.3*

Flushing Inn
1 Monad 2003; Holloway 1847, p603
2 SE Ad 21/10/1905

Forester's Arms
1 Rye/70/30
2 BUR/2/1/20
3 RC 9/7/1864
4 SE Ad 27/12/1884
5 SE Ad 10/03/1906

George Inn
1 Byng 1954
2 Vidler 1934
3 HP Clark 1861, p159

George Tap
1 Russell 8/2011

2 Rye 9/56
3 Rye 9/70
4 Ewart 1985, p82; SE 1872

Globe
1 AMS 5681/1/3
2 SE 10/01/1838
3 SE Ad 12/-7/1873
4 SE Ad 11/01/1908
5 SE Ad 21/02/1903
6 SE Ad 11/02/1905
7 SE Ad 12/11/1898

Greyhound
1 *London Gazette* 19/5/1863
2 Ewart 1985, p85
3 SE Ad 4/04/1891
4 DAP 325/1/7
5 SE Ad 24/6/05
6 SE Ad 10/03/1906

Hope Anchor
1 VID/2/2/14
2 SE Ad 14/06/1862
3 SE Ad 10/10/1874
4 SE Ad 1/02/1879
5 SE Ad 19/03/1881
6 SE Ad 2/07/1881
7 SE 10/06/1925

Jolly Sailor
1 Rye/14/34
2 Ewart 1985, p55
3 SE Ad 23/08/1879
4 SE Ad 28/08/1886
5 SE Ad 12/03/1910

Kings Arms
1 AMS 6128/1/4-29
2 SE Ad 7/04/1860
3 Rye/50/74
4 SE Ad 2/07/1859
5 SE Ad 28/06/1879
6 SE Ad 6/03/1886
7 6/02/1909

London Stout House
1. Rye/9/88, Rye/8/69
2. VID/5/2/17
3. *Rye Memories* vol 13, p27
4. Radcliff-Hall 1936
5. SE Ad 27/02/1892
6. DAP 325/1-7
7. SE Ad 7/03/1908

Mermaid Inn
1. Vidler 1934
2. Clark 1999
3. Holloway 1847
4. Jennings 2009
5. SE Ad 3/11/1894
6. SE Ad 26/01/1896
7. SE Ad 28/03/1908
8. SE 23/10/1931
9. SE 6/02/1948
10. SE 11/02/1955

Oak Inn
1. SE Ad 12/03/1881
2. SE Ad 6/02/1909
3. SE Ad 6/03/1909

Old Bell
1. AMS 5681/71/1-3
2. AMS 5681/71/7
3. SE Ad 10/02/1906
4. Russell 10/2011
5. Southerden 1928

Pipemaker's Arms
1. AMS 5681/51
2. Rye/14/29
3. Rye/8/125
4. Government Report 1852
5. RC 31/01/1863
6. SE Ad 18/02/1911
7. *Rye Memories* 'A Walk Along High Street'
8. SE 4/12/1925

Queen Adelaide
1. Rye/42/11

2. SE Ad 20/09/1862
3. RC 3/12/1864
4. SE Ad 6/12/1902
5. SE Ad 8/02/1908
6. SE Ad 1/09/1914
7. Whitbread's miniature inn signs 1949, 1st series no.12

Queens Head
1. Rye/70/29
2. AMS 5681/2/5
3. AMS 5681/2/8
4. AMS 5681/2/14
5. SE Ad 2/04/1859
6. SE Ad 29/01/1875
7. SE Ad -/12/1898
8. SE Ad 22/01/1916, 29/01/1916

Red Lion
1. Rye 70/23
2. Clark, 2011 p22
3. SWA 25/10/1756
4. SWA 2/01/1758
5. SWA 4/07/1757
6. Clark, 1861 p87
7. VID/2/2/59
8. RC 27/04/1872
9. RC 7/05/1874

Ship
1. ACC 8396/1/13
2. SE Ad 13/02/1892
3. Hyde, 2004 p78
4. VID/2/2/1
5. SE Ad 7/1/1888
6. SE Ad 25/03/1882
7. SE Ad 26/06/1886
8. SE Ad 13/02/1892
9. SE 2/02/1933

Standard Inn and the Swan
1. SE Ad 8/08/1879
2. RC 7/12/1867
3. RC op cit

4 SE Ad 10/02/1906

Tower
1 RC 24/03/1866
2 RC 30/03/1866
3 SE Ad 12/03/1910

Union Inn
1 PAB 256
2 op cit
3 VID/2/2/25

4 RC 27/8/1864
5 SE Ad 8/05/1881
6 *Adams Guide to Rye* 1934
7 www.ghostclub.org.uk
8 Spencer and Wells 1994 Ch 10

Ypres Castle Inn
1 VID 2/2/42
2 *Adams Guide to Rye* 1934
3 Taylor 2009 p114-117
4 SE Ad 12/08/1905

Bibliography

Books:

Bying, J. (1954) *The Torrington Diaries.* London: Eyre & Spottiswood.

Clark, H.P. (1861) *Clark's Guide and History of Rye, to which is added its political history, interspersed with many pleasing and interesting incidents.* Rye: Clark.

Clark, K.M. (1999) *Rye: A Short History.* Rye: Rye Heritage Centre.

Clark, K.M. (2011) *Smuggling in Rye and District.* Rye: Rye Museum.

Dunkling, L. and Wright, G. *(1987) A Dictionary of Pub Names.* London: R.K.P.

Ewart, P. (1985) *A poor man's Rye: the daily life of a local labouring family 1847–1930.* Canterbury: Peter Ewart.

Holloway, William. (1847) *History and Antiquities of the Ancient Town and Port of Rye.* London: John Russell Smith.

Jennings, L. (2009) *Field Paths and Green Lanes in Surrey and Sussex.* Carolina USA: Bibliolife.

Jennings, P. (2007) *The Local: A History of the English Pub.* Stroud: Tempus.

Monod, P.K. (2003) *The Murder of Mr Grebell.* London: New Haven.

Radclyffe-Hall, M. (1936) *The Sixth Beatitude.* London: Heineman.

Russell, D. (3/2011) *Register of Licensees for* Hastings & *St Leonards 1500–2010.* St Leonards-on-Sea: Lynda Russell.

Russell, D. (8/2011) *The Swan, Hastings 1523–1943.* St Leonards-on-Sea: Lynda Russell.

Russell, D. (10/2011) *The Pubs of Hastings & St Leonards 1800–2000, Second Edition.* St Leonards-on-Sea: Lynda Russell.

Spencer, J. and Wells, T. *(1995) Ghost Watching: The Ghosthunter's Handbook.* London: Virgin Books.

Taylor, A.R. (2009) *Played at the Pub: The Pub Games of Britain.* English Heritage.

Vidler, L.A. (1934) *A New History of Rye.* Hove: Combridges.

Newspapers:

London Gazette 1849, 1863.
Rye Chronicle 1863–1874.
South East Advertiser 1859–1862, 1875–1917.
Sussex Express 1837, 1917–1950.
Sussex Weekly Advertiser 1756–1788.

Other Sources:

Bloomfield, C. (2000) *Now and Then: A walk along Rye High Street.* Rye: Rye Local History Group.

Bradley, A.G. (nd but Comac 1930s) *Some British Inns, No.2. The Mermaid, Rye.* London: True Temperance Association.

HMSO Report from the Select Committee on the Rye Election Petition 1853.

Rye History Group. (1993–2010) *Newsletters.* Rye Museum.

Rye's Own, (1965–1973, 2000–2012) Volumes 1–11.

Rye Street Directories

Rye Town Guides

Southerden, D.G. (1928) *Sussex County Magazine, Volume 11, No. 8.* 'Smugglers Holes at Rye'.

Spink-Bagley, G. (1964) *Old Inns and Alehouses of Rye.* Rye Museum.

Thomas Peacock School Local History Group. *(1987–1999) Rye Memories, Volumes 1–24.*

Index